Wild Sea

Wild Sea

Eco-Wars and Surf Stories
from the Coast of the Californias

SERGE DEDINA

The University of Arizona Press
Tucson

The University of Arizona Press
© 2011 The Arizona Board of Regents
All rights reserved

www.uapress.arizona.edu

Library of Congress Cataloging-in-Publication Data
Dedina, Serge, 1964–
    Wild sea : eco-wars and surf stories from the coast of the Californias /
Serge Dedina.
        p. cm.
    Includes bibliographical references and index.
    ISBN 978-0-8165-2903-2 (pbk. : alk. paper)
    1. Coastal zone management—California. 2. Coastal zone management—
Mexico—Baja California (Peninsula) 3. Coastal ecology—California.
4. Coastal ecology—Mexico—Baja California (Peninsula) 5. Land use—
California. 6. Land use—Mexico—Baja California (Peninsula) I. Title.
    HT393.C2D43 2011
    333.91'709722—dc22

                                                              2010039338

Publication of this book is made possible in part by a grant
from WILDCOAST.

Manufactured in the United States of America on acid-free,
archival-quality paper containing a minimum of 30 percent
post-consumer waste and processed chlorine free.

16   15   14   13   12   11   6   5   4   3   2   1

Contents

Maps

Illustrations

Acknowledgments

Being a full-time coastal conservationist can be a frustrating and rewarding experience. I could not do this work without the backing of the passionate and dedicated team at Wildcoast—board and staff—who help make my work possible. I am also lucky to have had the longtime support of Anne Earhart and Beto Bedolfe of the Marisla Foundation; Jim Sandler and Sergio Knaebel of the Sandler Family Foundation; Smoky and Kim Bayless; Paul Eichen and Susan Flieder of the Orca Fund; Linda Wallace-Gray of the Wallace Research Foundation; Richard Kiy of the International Community Foundation; Julie Packard and Richard Cudney of the David and Lucile Packard Foundation; Sean Smith, Paul Naude, Dick Baker (rest in peace), and the SIMA Environmental Fund board; the board and executive team at REI; the Resources Law Group and Resources Legacy Fund Foundation team; and the California Endowment. A California Wellness Foundation Sabbatical Award provided me with the opportunity to work on this project.

Among the many colleagues and friends who continue to encourage and inspire me are Chris Patterson, Jeff Knox, Greg Tate, Richard Abrams, Mike Richardson, Kem Nunn, Ken Weiss, Greg Abbott, Jamie Mitchell, Garth Murphy, Mark Rennecker, Chet Tchozewski, Steve Merrill, Kimball Taylor, Oscar Romo, Scott Hulet, Lori Saldaña, Alex Dick Reid, Teri Fenner, Trace Funderburk, Patricia and Mike McCoy, Dick Russell, Javier Villavicencio, John Elwell, Brian Bouch, Patricia and Gabriel Weisz, David Milch, Bill Powers, Rory Cox, Randy Olsen, Isidro Arce, Mark Massara, Joel Reynolds, Jacob Scherr, the IB and Los Cirios crews, Luis Bourrillon, Miguel Vargas, Gustavo Danemann, Fernando Ochoa, Susan Jordan, Maná, Robert Garcia, Terry Gibson, Jim Moriarty and Matt McClain and the entire Surfrider Foundation crew, Will Henry, Dean LaTourette, El Hijo del Santo, and the staff at the San Diego Zoo's Institute for Conservation Research. I am thankful to have spent time talking story with Allen "Dempsey" Holder and Bernard Nietschmann, both California watermen who have since passed away.

A special thanks goes to Ambassador Homero Aridjis and Betty Aridjis for their friendship and leadership in coastal protection and to Homero for permission to reprint our two coauthored articles, "How Saving Whales Advances Democracy" and "Protecting Mexico's Natural Heritage." I would also like to thank the Aguilar, Mayoral, Holder, and Knox families for sharing their lives lived by the sea.

Thanks to *California Coast and Ocean*, *Surfer's Journal*, *Voice of San Diego*, *Longboard Magazine*, *Surfshot*, *Los Angeles Times*, *San Diego Union-Tribune*, *Grist*, *Surfing*, and *Mains'l Haul* for permission to publish these dispatches. I am grateful to Jason Murray, Ralph Lee Hopkins, and the Surfrider Foundation for permission to reprint photos and campaign art. Diana Castañeda, Katie Westfall, Zach Plopper, Michel Dedina, Emily Young, Fay Crevoshay, Ben Marcus, Drew Kampion, Sally Bennett, Stephanie Batt, and an anonymous reviewer provided much-appreciated editorial assistance and input. Lore Dach prepared maps and illustrations. For surfing terms in the Glossary, I consulted Matt Warshaw, *The Encyclopedia of Surfing* (Orlando, FL: Harcourt, 2003) and Zach Plopper, a Wildcoast staff member, surf writer, and professional surfer. Thanks to Allyson Carter, editor in chief of the University of Arizona Press, and the wonderful University of Arizona Press staff for their support. I am also fortunate and thankful for the love, patience, and encouragement of Emily, Daniel, Israel, and my parents.

Abbreviations

ASR	Action Sport Retail Expo
CONANP	National Natural Protected Area Commission of Mexico
ESSA	Mexican Salt Exporting Company
FONATUR	National Tourism Fund of Mexico
GAO	U.S. Government Accountability Office
IBWC	International Boundary and Water Commission
LNG	Liquefied natural gas
NAFTA	North American Free Trade Agreement
NGO	Nongovernmental organization
NRDC	Natural Resources Defense Council
PRI	Institutional Revolutionary Party
SIMA	Surf Industry Manufacturing Association
TCA	Transportation Corridor Agencies

Wild Sea

Introduction

Conflict and Conservation on the
Coast of the Californias

A surf trip anywhere in Baja California, Mexico, used to be all about finding uncrowded waves, clean water, and a no-worries escape from Southern California. Due to the plague of pollution and narco-violence, however, now those conditions can only be found south of Punta Baja, more than two hundred miles south of the U.S.–Mexico border. There, the last remaining wild Pacific coastline is still dotted with small fishing settlements. There is almost no pollution. Coastal access is unimpeded. Security means wearing rubber wetsuit booties to avoid stubbing your toe while walking out to surf cobblestone pointbreaks.

In contrast, the peninsula north of El Rosario is the stomping ground of modern pirates—corporate henchmen, land speculators, resource poachers, and corrupt government officials—whose destructive activities have forever altered the coast of the Californias.

As I rounded the Ensenada harbor on a misty morning after spending four days surveying the remote coastline of the central Pacific coast of Baja, I was faced with the physical evidence of how fast a once spectacular and public coastline has been transformed into one of the world's worst examples of unplanned, no-access, and polluted coastal corridors.

San Miguel, one of the last remaining surf spots in the Ensenada area, had been proposed as the site of a new yacht harbor. Gates barricaded the Salsipuedes campground north of Ensenada. The lights of the Sempra Energy (an American company) liquefied natural gas (LNG) terminal blinked in the distance. Sempra built the plant in Mexico to bypass oversight and public opposition north of the border.

I passed Rosarito Beach, the hangout of drug cartel gunmen. Not a tourist was in sight along its streets, lined with garish narco-deco high-rise condominiums and hotels. The wave of narco-violence, combined with the implosion of the global economy, cleared Baja California of tourists. Defunct coastal zone high-rise hotel and condo projects litter the coastal zone between Tijuana and Ensenada. Other projects, such as the ill-fated Trump Ocean Resort Baja, were abandoned after grading began.

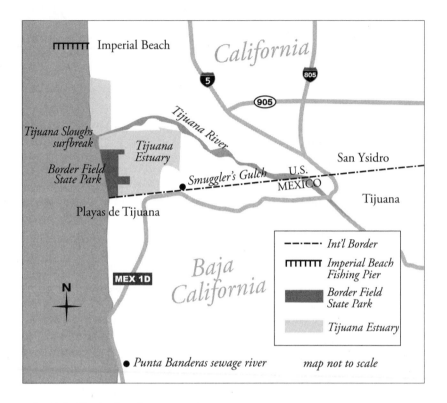

The U.S.–Mexico border

A few miles north of Rosarito, I caught a glimpse of the river of sewage at Punta Banderas. Up to 30 million gallons of wastewater spew onto the beach every day, contaminating the coastline for miles. As I passed the last tollgate on the Pacific Coast Highway before entering the canyons of western Tijuana, I looked across the newly erected Homeland Security border wall to the United States and the Sloughs, a mythical big-wave surfing spot. The Sloughs is offshore from Imperial Beach, my hometown, where Tijuana River pollution closed local beaches for more than 1,600 days over the past decade.

The half-baked development schemes and horrific pollution in Baja California are a mirror image of the past and present of the environmental problems and battles in Southern California for the past forty years. Whether in response to the 1969 oil spill in Santa Barbara, the loss of the Killer Dana surf spot in Dana Point to a yacht marina, or efforts to restrict high-rise towers along the Southern California coast, time and time again, citizen groups have mobilized to defend the coastline that sustains them.

This book is designed to offer a glimpse into the battles we have faced in attempting to conserve the best of our coastal heritage in both California and Baja California. My aim is to document the campaigns that I have been involved with to preserve the last wild coastline and marine wildlife of the Californias and to provide a look at the roots of the binational coastal culture of the Californias.

I have not written a neutral academic monograph on coastal management. Rather, I provide a passionate and unapologetic defense of our coastal heritage in the Californias. Many of these dispatches were written in the midst of campaigning to provide a sense of urgency to the public about the fate of our coast. Few people realize how close we came to losing important pieces of the coastline of the Californias to badly planned and doomed-to-fail development.

In Part I, "The Baja California Peninsula," I discuss the cultural and political ecology of ocean lifeways and conservation battles in Baja California. From the Kanakas, or Hawaiians, who were the first to ride waves on wooden planks along the Baja California peninsula, to the fishing families of Baja's Pacific coast, I describe livelihoods and histories that have almost disappeared. Twentieth-century Baja California had more in common with the nineteenth century than our current one does. When the development boom hit Baja at the end of the twentieth century, developers, government officials, corporate titans, and speculators arrived in remote fishing villages claiming to hold the keys to instant riches and megaprojects that ended up no more real than mirages that shimmer in the salt flats of San Ignacio Lagoon.

In Part II, "The U.S.–Mexico Border," I document efforts to defend the natural environment of a region that is neither Mexico nor the United States. Sometimes it is a no-man's-land where badly planned projects and coastal con artists flourish. I discuss a successful attempt to stop Chevron-Texaco from building a liquefied natural gas terminal at Mexico's Coronado Islands. I also document the horrendous flow of sewage onto the beaches of the San Diego–Tijuana region and the efforts of nefarious schemers to profit from the pollution crisis. The contradictions of the massive earthen border barrier hastily erected by the U.S. Department of Homeland Security are illustrated to show that not all border problems emanate from Mexico to the United States. I look at the pop culture personalities behind Tijuana's punk rock and *lucha libre* (Mexican wrestling) scenes that give the tumultuous U.S.–Mexico border where I live its vibrancy and energy and influenced my own activism.

In Part III, "Southern California," I document the pop culture–themed environmental fight over the proposal to build a highway through San Onofre State Beach to show how a coastal lifestyle centered on experiencing the flow of riding waves, skateboarding, and other adrenaline-inducing pastimes is helping to shape the environmental movement. Popular culture is a necessary mantle in which to wrap campaigns to preserve the coast: it makes the environmental movement relevant. This became evident when the Surfrider Foundation ran through a litany of retro rock themes—from the Sex Pistols' "God Save the Queen" to AC/DC's "Back in Black"—to promote the Save Trestles campaign. That effort attracted six thousand people to public hearings to protest plans to build a toll road through San Onofre State Beach.

Because many of these dispatches were written before the fate of the coastal development projects I fought had been decided, the epilogue provides a discussion of the results of campaigns I was privileged to help plan and carry out (which, for the most part, we won). A discussion about how we can reclaim our coast, along with additional updated information throughout the chapters on the status of the issues and campaigns, is also included.

While these stories and essays were being written, the U.S. and global economy were on a manic-depressive bender with the highs and lows that either boost efforts to develop the coast or stop construction in midstream. But regardless of whether the Dow is riding high or government coffers are full, conservationists must work full time with coastal residents to put an end to the mostly unnecessary and often bizarre development projects that threaten our lives and livelihoods. Battles over natural resources and the boom-and-bust times that exacerbate them are not new: these conflicts have existed since Europeans first sailed the mythical coast of a California that they believed would be an earthly paradise.

The Pristine Myth

For years, tourists, government officials, and residents of Baja California operated under what geographer William Denevan calls the "pristine myth," the belief that the landscape of Baja California (along with that of the rest of the Americas) was "a world of barely perceptible human disturbance."[1] This myth led locals and outsiders in the twentieth century to believe that the Baja California peninsula—old Baja—was a pristine land with unlimited natural resources, too vast and remote to be touched by the forces of modernity.[2] They ignored the historic plunder of its natural treasures and landscape. This myth continues to cloud the vision of Mexican government planners, investors, and tourists, who are blind to the reality of environmental degradation: they are blinded by the mythology of "old Baja," which has long since disappeared.

Since 1579, when Sir Francis Drake sailed the Pacific coast of Baja California in search of treasure-laden Spanish galleons to plunder, the peninsula has been the subject of predations by a long line of pirates—buccaneers, resource poachers, speculators, corrupt government officials, filibusterers, mining companies, whalers, foreign governments, and fishing companies. They sacked the natural resources of the Baja California peninsula for the glory of king, country, and personal fortune.[3] Baja California has been the setting for spectacular booms and even more sordid tales of bust. None was more spectacular than the story of filibusterer William Walker, who invaded the peninsula and established the very short-lived Republic of Lower California in 1853.[4] In the 1860s, President Benito Juárez gave away much of the peninsula's coastline to American speculators through generous concessions. From the 1840s through the 1870s, American whalers came close to exterminating gray whales. Through the end of the nineteenth century, hunters employed by foreign mining companies nearly wiped out pronghorn antelope and bighorn sheep to keep miners fed. The disregard for Baja California by Mexican federal authorities was such that dictator Porfirio Diaz even allowed the U.S. Navy to use Magdalena Bay, a gray whale birthing site, as a bombardment-training site during the first decade of the twentieth century.[5]

Not until the late 1930s did the Mexican government, under President Lázaro Cárdenas, repulse foreign companies and pirates in their attempts to control the peninsula's natural resources and its territory. Cárdenas and his successors established large land collectives (*ejidos*) and the federal government–sanctioned fishing cooperative villages that dot the Pacific coastline today.[6]

The Baja Boom

The period of nationalization of the Baja California peninsula coastline took place from the 1930s to the 1980s. During that time, the federal government handed out millions of acres of what seemed to be worthless desert coastline to ejidos. The redistribution of land came to an end when President Carlos Salinas and the new era of free market or neoliberal Mexico arrived in 1988. One of the most significant policy acts of Salinas (who was to become the great villain of twentieth-century Mexico for causing the economic meltdown of 1994, a quaint precursor to the global meltdown of 2008) was changing the Mexican constitution to allow once-collectivist ejidatarios to become private property owners.

For the first time, due to the privatization of ejidos, the white sand beaches and pristine coastal desert of Baja California that had been locked out of the real estate market could be purchased. This resulted in the "Baja Boom," a race by con men, speculators, and multinational corporations to buy up and develop the coastline of the Baja California peninsula from 1995 to 2008.[7]

Instead of landless migrants racing across the plains in search of a plot of land, as in the Oklahoma Land Rush, tinted-window Chevy Suburbans driven by real estate hustlers and the agents of multinationals showed up at the ranchos and fish camps of the Baja California peninsula. They offered sweet deals to semiliterate and unsophisticated ejidatarios for their coastal properties. It was a Mexican version of *Wall Street* meets *The Grapes of Wrath*. One aging fisherman in the central Pacific coast, desolate over the death of his wife, sold a pristine Pacific coastal headland to a trucking company owner for $5,000 and then drank himself to death.

The boom detonated with the announcement in early 1995 that the Mitsubishi Corporation planned to develop a 500,000-acre industrial salt harvesting facility adjacent to San Ignacio Lagoon, the world's last undeveloped gray whale birthing lagoon. As a result, conservationists, who had ignored Baja California in the mistaken belief that the peninsula could never be developed, rushed in to defend it. I was among a coalition of activists and local fishermen who campaigned against the project.

The Baja Boom reached its zenith during the rule of President Vicente Fox, from 2000 to 2006. During those years, I dreaded reading the morning newspaper, for fear of facing another headline about the latest coastal development proposed for a Baja California peninsula beach, lagoon, or island renowned for its endangered wildlife and spectacular beauty.

Among the proposed projects was a plan by President Fox to build a network of marinas and resorts, the Escalera Nautica (Nautical Ladder), at over twenty of the most remote beaches in the peninsula and northwestern Mexico. Fox announced the project a year after his predecessor

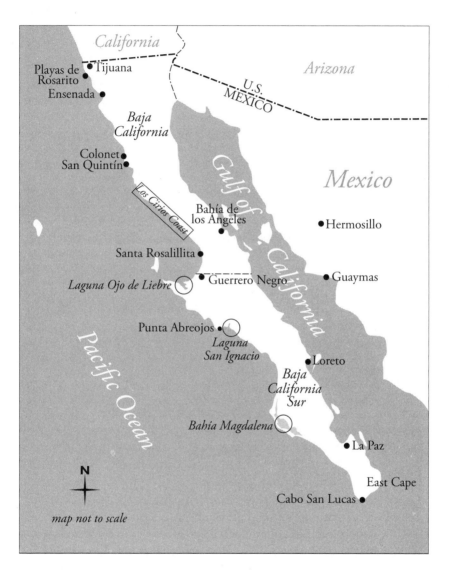

The Baja California peninsula

cancelled the salt project. Beaches along Baja's central Pacific coast, barely on the radar even for surfers due to their isolation, were being offered up as future marina locations. Hand-painted signs posted along Baja California's Transpeninsular Highway announced land for sale at the proposed marina sites.

Within months of the announcement of the marina plans, workers began dynamiting a hillside adjacent to a wetland at an isolated Pacific coastal ranch just north of the fishing village of Santa Rosalillita, four hundred miles south of the U.S.–Mexico border. Soon after, an assortment of raggedy skip loaders dumped the boulders from the new quarry into the surf at Santa Rosalillita, a locale known for its shallow embayment, sand dunes, perfect point surf, and high winds favored by wind and kite surfers. Tourism officials believed that sailors would dock their yachts at Santa Rosalillita and have them hauled out of the water and trucked east across the peninsula to the sleepy fishing village of Bahía de los Angeles on the Sea of Cortez. As a result of its new rock jetties, the forgotten lobster village of Santa Rosalillita became ground zero for Fox's ambitious tourist plan. The president even helicoptered in to visit the future marina in 2003.

At the same time, some of the world's largest oil and energy companies—such as Shell, Chevron-Texaco, Sempra, Marathon Oil, and El Paso—proposed building liquefied natural gas terminals between Tijuana and Ensenada. Just offshore from Tijuana, Chevron-Texaco planned a $700 million LNG facility at the Coronado Islands (just south of the U.S.–Mexico border), a refuge for elephant seals and a threatened species of seabird, the Xantus's murrelet. In the dusty and coastal sage scrub-covered coast of Colonet, Taiwanese investors and speculators headed by former Baja California governor Ernesto Ruffo planned a new megaport to rival the Port of Los Angeles in California.

The explosion of narco-cash and global credit market funny money also facilitated the proliferation of hotels, condos, and vacation homes from Tijuana to Los Cabos. Developers marketed what once would have been a routine golf course development, Loreto Bay, as "one of the world's most sustainably developed resorts." However, the developers, TSD Partners, suspended construction activities on June 8, 2009, due to what interim company president Embree Bedsole called "the challenging situation in the international real estate and financial markets." Ironically, what was the region's premier private-sector "green" development project is now under the management of Mexico's National Tourism Fund (FONATUR), the same agency that promoted the Nautical Ladder.[8]

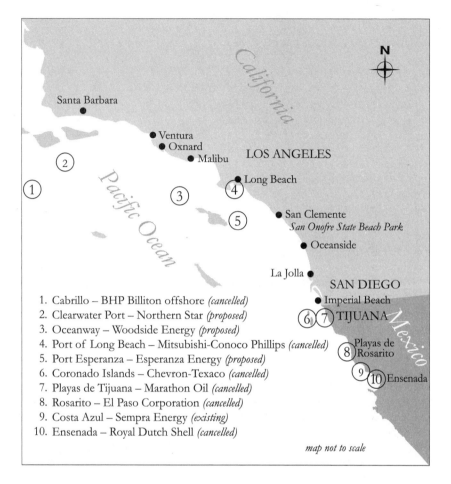

1. Cabrillo – BHP Billiton offshore *(cancelled)*
2. Clearwater Port – Northern Star *(proposed)*
3. Oceanway – Woodside Energy *(proposed)*
4. Port of Long Beach – Mitsubishi-Conoco Phillips *(cancelled)*
5. Port Esperanza – Esperanza Energy *(proposed)*
6. Coronado Islands – Chevron-Texaco *(cancelled)*
7. Playas de Tijuana – Marathon Oil *(cancelled)*
8. Rosarito – El Paso Corporation *(cancelled)*
9. Costa Azul – Sempra Energy *(existing)*
10. Ensenada – Royal Dutch Shell *(cancelled)*

map not to scale

The proposed LNG terminals in Southern California and northern Baja California

Property owners desperate for cash in Baja even posted "developer wanted" signs along the highway. In the once-tranquil East Cape region, armed guards patrolled white sand beaches against the intrusion of local residents. Thugs even attacked one activist who attempted to photograph condo development in La Paz's El Mogote peninsula. Billboards for high-rise towers and luxury spa hotels began to pop up everywhere. Soon Baja became the new playground for stars such as Jennifer Anniston and Jessica Alba and for hordes of wannabe international glitterati.

Environmental activist Peter Patterson confronts guards at the El Mogote resort development site in Baja California Sur.

A "developer wanted" sign in northern Baja California just south of Tijuana.

This cavalcade of projects galvanized formerly tame marine biologists, conservationists, businessmen, and tourism operators. Many who vociferously opposed these new development projects had previously shunned political activism for fear of angering the Mexican government. This rise in environmental activism after 2000 coincided with the disassembling of Mexico's one-party state under the sway of the Institutional Revolutionary Party (PRI). In the past, government officials often labeled environmental activists *vendepatrias* (traitors) or worse. Antilogging activists Rodolfo Montiel and Teodoro Cabrera in the southern Mexican state of Guerrero, for example, were arrested and tortured. Their attorney Digna Ochoa was assassinated.[9]

Many tame conservationists, who had previously criticized outspoken environmental leaders such as poet and Group of 100 president Homero Aridjis for his relentless public condemnation of government development schemes, joined him in opposing the Escalera Nautica project. For the first time, conservationists learned how to file lawsuits, build grassroots support, lobby Mexico's Congress, and make their voices heard through the international and newly independent Mexican media. The irony of the Baja Boom is that it forced Mexico's environmental movement to take advantage of and use the new tools of democracy.

The U.S.–Mexico Border

From 2000 to 2008, the seaside Border Field State Park, which divides Tijuana from San Diego a few miles from Imperial Beach, became ground zero for developers and government agencies who tried to use the vacuum of governance in Mexico and the United States to push through shady projects. Two shadowy businessmen from San Diego and Tijuana spent more than $20 million in lobbying fees and campaign contributions in an attempt to receive a $600 million sole-source no-bid U.S. federal government contract to build a sewage treatment plant in eastern Tijuana. They promised that their plant would be the magic bullet to solve the complex problem of sewage that cascades out of the unplumbed shantytowns throughout Tijuana and into the salt marshes of Border Field and the Tijuana Estuary.

In 2005, the U.S. Department of Homeland Security began the construction of a massive earthen, concrete, and metal security barrier that would extend through Border Field State Park and along the border from San Ysidro to the Pacific Ocean (and initiated construction of a

Constructing a barrier along the U.S.–Mexico border just west of the San Ysidro border crossing.

Storm-related flooding at Smuggler's Gulch on the U.S.–Mexico border just west of the San Ysidro border crossing.

similar barrier along many portions of the entire U.S.–Mexico border). To facilitate construction, the Department of Homeland Security ordered the barrier to be free of any environmental or public review. Because the Homeland Security Department placed little emphasis on engineering the barrier with sufficient erosion control measures, winter rains caused massive mudslides that inundated local ranches and stables and filled portions of the federally protected Tijuana Estuary in the United States with silt. Joe Sharkey, a *New York Times* reporter whom I took on a tour of the border and the northern Baja coast, said of the massive amphitheater of dirt that Homeland Security dumped in Smuggler's Gulch, a few miles from the Pacific, "They did better engineering in 8th century China."[10]

The political result of all this development in the border region and in Baja California was an unplanned bilateral exchange of activists. California environmentalists descended upon the Baja California peninsula to denounce U.S.-financed coastal development. Meanwhile, Mexican conservationists and natural resource officials condemned what they viewed as the new Berlin Wall on their northern border. Ironically, in previous years, Mexican and U.S. officials and conservation organizations cooperated to preserve endangered wildlife such as the Sonoran pronghorn, ocelot, jaguarundi, and jaguar along the U.S.–Mexico border.[11]

Southern California

In Southern California, the passage of the California Coastal Act in 1972 came too late to halt the paving over of the tender coastal salt marshes, coastal bluffs covered with native pines, and river valleys filled with deer, mountain lions, and Native American ceremonial sites. This magical coastline is described by Garth Murphy in his novel of California, *The Indian Lover*, as "the boundless freedom of an endless horizon . . . where a dozen blue-green chunks of the tumbling California coastal range jutted majestically from the frothy sea"; today it is a sea of highways, coastal mansions, piers, and parking lots.[12]

A new generation of pirates has emerged in coastal Southern California. They are the bureaucrats, union officials, corporate lobbyists, CEOs, oil company barons, and elected officials who view the natural coastline and ocean of California as an area to be plundered rather than preserved. They do their best to rid Southern California of the shoreline that makes the coast the oxygen that fuels the state's vibrant culture and economy.

From 1972 to 2000, the efforts of environmentalists to protect the California shoreline mainly focused on influencing the California Coastal Commission to prevent the further destruction of the remaining public-access beaches, salt marshes, and coastal river valleys. From 2001 to 2008, as a result of the explosion of energy development and hotel, condo, and housing construction in the United States, the landscape of coastal protection suddenly changed: for activists to keep pace with development threats to the coast became almost impossible.

Battling the Pirates

Through it all, the residents of the coastline of the Californias—fishermen, surfers, birdwatchers, biologists, and everyday people who believe that our coastal heritage is all that we have left of "lost California"—fought back.[13] In the mangrove lagoons of southern Baja's Magdalena Bay, fishing co-op members battled resource poachers who do double duty as drug runners and sea turtle killers. The fishermen of the Pacific village of Punta Abreojos attempted to halt these poachers from carrying out nighttime raids on their lobster grounds and abalone beds. These fishermen also pitched in to stop the Mitsubishi salt project and an Escalera marina planned for their beach.

Along the U.S.–Mexico border, in Imperial Beach, a motley group of surfers inspired by Allen "Dempsey" Holder, a legendary surfer who pioneered surfing the outer reef waves of the Sloughs, joined forces with Border Patrol agents, U.S. Navy Seals, the residents of the upscale village of Coronado, and the inhabitants of the poorest *colonias* of Tijuana to search for their own solutions to the international sewage crisis.

Corporations such as Chevron-Texaco and BHP Billiton planned a network of portside and offshore LNG terminals along the U.S.–Mexico border and in Southern California with the support of the once-green Governor Arnold Schwarzenegger and the George W. Bush administration. Meanwhile, the cash-strapped City of San Diego proposed spending up to one million dollars to dredge a tiny beach in San Diego's upscale enclave of La Jolla to rid the area of a small population of what were supposed to be federally protected harbor seals.

At Trestles Beach, just south of San Clemente (located between the convergence zone of laid-back, liberal San Diego and politically conservative Orange County), Native Americans, surfers, and environmentalists fought to halt the construction of a toll road through San Onofre State

A colonia in Tijuana.

Beach, a highway project proposed by the politically powerful Orange County–based Transportation Corridor Agencies (TCA).

My experiences with the ocean culture of the Californias and witnessing firsthand the conflict between developers and coastal residents provide the material for the dispatches in this book. I grew up in Imperial Beach, a blue-collar beach city located at the edge of the Tijuana River valley on the U.S.–Mexico border. The valley is an area that Kem Nunn in his novel *The Tijuana Straits* argues is neither "America nor Mexico but rather a country unto itself." He likens the valley to the "forbidden zone in *Planet of the Apes*, a vast wasteland caught between the gates of two cities, a repository of fringe dwellers and secret histories."[14] The Tijuana River valley is where I played Little League, threw my bike over the dilapidated U.S.–Mexico border fence to cruise around Playas de Tijuana with my friends, and clambered over hillsides to find abandoned World War II bunkers.

Imperial Beach and the border are where I learned to surf and where I became an accidental environmentalist. My childhood and teen years were spent successfully battling former Imperial Beach mayor Brian

Bilbray, now a U.S. congressman representing San Diego's affluent North County, to keep him from transforming the Tijuana Estuary into a yacht harbor. I also worked with other coastal activists to stop Bilbray from destroying our surfing beach through the construction of a federally funded breakwater project. That effort became the first victory for the then fledgling Surfrider Foundation, now an organization with more than 45,000 members. When pollution from Tijuana cascaded onto our beaches, I sought Third World–appropriate solutions to the border sewage crisis; massive centralized sewage plants typical of First World countries do little to treat the sewage of unplumbed neighborhoods in the developing world.

In Imperial Beach, I worked as an ocean lifeguard and interviewed legendary surfer Dempsey Holder and surfing pioneers such as Lorrin Harrison and Ron Drummond. From those conversations, I learned that our baseline for appreciating the natural features of the coast had radically changed. This "shifting baseline" (in the words of marine biologist Randy Olson) caused many Southern California residents to believe that the current state of a polluted and overdeveloped coastline was normal and to be expected.[15] They did not know that only decades earlier, Southern California's coastline had been filled with miles of salt marshes and an ocean so abundant with fish that giant black sea bass could be caught from fishing piers. Talking to surfing veterans and old fishermen, I gained an appreciation for the coastal treasures we had lost and the imperative for preserving what remains.

After I started surfing, at the age of thirteen in 1977, I frequently traveled south of the border to surf the once-spectacular coastline between Tijuana and Ensenada. Those quick trips turned into longer expeditions with my father and friends to central Pacific Baja in a beat-up olive green 1964 six-volt Volkswagen van. We found friendly fishermen and pristine beaches and surfed perfect waves. Those same beaches that I surfed later became the focal point for the Mexican government's Escalera Nautica megamarina project.

In Baja California, I befriended generous fishing and ranching families who live a hardscrabble life miles from the nearest paved road. However, underneath the smiles and warm *abrazos* (hugs) I encountered was a palpable tension. It was the result of the intense conflicts between the residents of the fish camps, lagoons, and beaches of the Baja California peninsula and the poachers, corporate henchmen, and government officials attempting to purloin their resources and livelihoods.

Four years living in El Salvador, Peru, Spain, and Morocco taught me that natural resource destruction is a contributing cause of poverty. I also learned how the absence of democracy and the rule of law contribute to the degradation of the coast and ocean. These experiences, combined with my history of grassroots activism along the U.S.–Mexico border, caused me to realize that only by galvanizing and working with coastal communities can environmental battles be won.

My childhood activism, surfing, travels abroad, and passion for environmental justice turned into graduate research on the geography of coastal conservation and development along the U.S.–Mexico border and in Baja California. I also spent two years living in Baja California with my wife, Emily, to carry out doctoral research on gray whale conservation. That research experience turned into a career as a professional coastal conservationist.

Immediately after completing graduate school in 1996, I was hired by The Nature Conservancy to develop a conservation program for Baja California and the Sea of Cortez. During my three years with The Nature Conservancy, I assisted in the development of the 510,000-acre Loreto Bay National Park in the Sea of Cortez, helped initiate an effort to permanently protect Isla Espíritu Santo off of the city of La Paz, and learned the fundamentals of nonprofit management. That fruitful experience gave me the ability in 2000 to partner with sea turtle biologist Wallace J. Nichols to start Wildcoast, a binational conservation organization located in Imperial Beach.

I have spent much of my time as a conservationist in Baja California, meandering the rutted and rocky dirt roads in an effort to preserve coastal and marine ecosystems and endangered wildlife. During a kayaking trip in San Ignacio Lagoon, my wife and I found the carapaces of slaughtered and endangered East Pacific green turtles left there by the infamous poacher Gordo Fischer. That discovery helped me to understand that sea turtles were in big trouble in Baja. Later, Wildcoast carried out a sustained campaign in Mexico to stop the illegal trade in sea turtle meat and eggs.

Thanks to my friendship with fishermen in San Ignacio Lagoon, I learned of plans by the Mitsubishi Corporation to build the San Ignacio Salt Project. That tip was the seed that started an international campaign to stop Mitsubishi.[16] Just south of the Bajamar Golf Resort in northern Baja California, surf photographer Jason Murray and I witnessed bulldozers destroy Harry's, a surf spot once featured on the cover of *Surfer* magazine.

Because in the binational world in which I live and work, nature cannot be separated from culture, I learned that in order to save endangered species such as sea turtles and sharks in Mexico, my colleagues and I had to adapt the cultural symbolism and values that give meaning to everyday life there. Hence we fused efforts to stop the cultural tradition of sea turtle meat and turtle egg consumption with messages related to religious figures (Pope John Paul II and priests), Mexican wrestlers, rock stars, and soccer players.

We even convinced *Playboy* cover girl Dorismar to join our efforts. An image of the Argentine playmate, posed in a sexy bikini, urged men to refrain from eating sea turtle eggs "because real men know it doesn't make them more potent." A shark conservation campaign in Mexico was themed around "El Rey Tiburon" (The Shark King), a popular song of Maná, Mexico's reigning rock superstars.

North of the border, in Southern California, I joined coastal residents attempting to hold on to the small patches of open space and pristine beaches that remain. During the campaign to preserve San Onofre State Beach, I assisted activists attempting to preserve a vestige of old California from the depredation of elected officials such as Governor Schwarzenegger. I also began to work in areas such as southern San Diego's Otay River valley to acquire and restore riparian habitat to provide recreational opportunities and healthy open space for some of the region's lowest-income communities.

The dispatches in this book foretell the types of battles and issues we will face when addressing one of the principal dilemmas of our coast and ocean: how we preserve and restore what remains of critical ecosystems; how we expand our movement to include communities outside the mostly wealthy coastal enclaves of Southern California; and how we turn back the clock of climate change. This is more imperative than ever because there is no greater gift than the refreshing waters of our aquatic playground and life-support system that ignores national borders.

Part I

The Baja California Peninsula

The attractions that the region holds for tourists are the
. . . wildness and loneliness of the land coupled with the
unspoiled character of its inhabitants.

—Homer Aschmann, *The Central Desert of Baja California:
Ecology and Demography*

1

The First Surfers in Baja California

Although California surfers like to think of themselves as the pioneers of surfing in Baja California, native Cochimí and Hawaiian surfriders preceded them by over a century. The indigenous inhabitants of Isla Cedros used rafts made from driftwood, native softwood timber, and tule reeds for hunting sea otters, fishing, and navigating the treacherous area between the island and the villages of the Central Desert region. Seri fishermen of the Sea of Cortez often paddled their elegant narrow rafts, made of bundled tules, while standing up. Their paddling technique was similar to balancing atop a stand-up paddle surfboard, especially in the often-choppy sea conditions around the Midriff Islands.[1]

Disease had wiped out much of Baja California's indigenous population by the 1850s, when American and European whalers, often carrying Hawaiian or Kanaka crew members, began sailing its coast in search of gray whales.[2] The whaling ships sailed from Hawaii to San Francisco and down to Mexico. Captain Charles Scammon, who hunted whales with Kanaka crewmen for many years along Baja's Pacific coast, provided the earliest account of wave riding in the peninsula.

In late 1857, two whaling ships, Scammon's *Boston* and the *Marin*, anchored off the entrance to Laguna Ojo de Liebre (now called Scammon's Lagoon), searching for a passage across the shallow bar into the lagoon, where gray whales annually calve at the end of their migration south. The scouts located a passage into the lagoon. Because the whales had not yet arrived, the crews of both brigs spent their time attending to chores and searching the deserted coast for firewood. During one such shore detail, the ship's carpenter became careless while bathing and capsized his boat. He endangered three other boats that were made fast, just outside the surfline. Fearing for his life, he swam for shore and left the boats drifting out to sea. Captain Scammon recalled,

> The alarm was given to the party on shore, and it was a disheartening sight to behold the four boats drifting through the breakers,

for everyone knew that without them our voyage would be fruitless. There were several Kanakas among the crew, who immediately saw the necessity of saving the boats, and selecting pieces of plank, to be used as "surf-boards," put off through the rollers to rescue them, when the anchor, which had been dragging all the while, brought up, and the current swept both carpenter and Kanakas out of reach. They then made for the shore, which all of them regained in an exhausted condition, except the carpenter who was never seen again.[3]

One can only speculate whether these "planks" were actually surfboards brought by the crew for recreational use from Hawaii, where surfing had a long history. One wonders, too, whether the Hawaiians also took advantage of any free time while at San Juanico Bight to the south, a popular anchorage for whalers, to ride the surf of Punta Pequeña or Scorpion Bay, today famed for its perfect point waves.

2

Magdalena Bay's People of the Mangroves

Carrying out field conservation programs in Baja California requires working closely with resident fishermen and their families. My first forays into Magdalena Bay with my wife, Emily, involved lengthy field trips with fishermen and whale-watching guides on their daily routines. We wanted to learn as much as possible about their attitudes and the details of their livelihoods. Without such information, developing successful programs and policies to conserve the diverse and rich ecosystems of Baja California would be impossible.

Standing next to his shoreline *palapa*, Francisco "Chico" Sarabia explained how to fillet stingray. "You cut the meat here," he said, pointing to the center of the fish he had drawn in the sand. "You have to be careful or you wind up with this in your leg." He showed me a three-inch barb.

A few days earlier, a large ray had stuck him through his rubber boot. "They get me once in a while. It isn't so bad," he told me with a grin. Having endured the intense pain of stingray barbs several times, I was not sure I believed him.

The people of the mangroves live hidden by the barrier islands of Magdalena Bay, which stretch for over a hundred miles along the southern coast of the Baja California peninsula. With one of the richest biological and cultural marine environments on the Pacific coast of North America, Magdalena Bay provides a glimpse of what that Baja California peninsula once was.

Dense stands of mangroves provide a nearly impenetrable defense for flocks of migratory birds. Gray whale mothers and their young spend the winter in the shallow channels. Sea lions inhabit the rocky coves of the barrier islands. East Pacific green turtles slowly recovering from near extinction feed in the shallow interior lagoons of the immense bay.

In Magdalena Bay, people fish, hunt, farm, raise livestock, and collect plants across hundreds of square miles of water and land. Descendants of the peninsula's first European and Mexican settlers, pirates, whalers, and more-recent arrivals pass on knowledge about their aquatic backyard to family and friends. Without such knowledge, making a living from the once-abundant but now dramatically declining natural resources of Magdalena Bay would be impossible.

During my doctoral research on the conservation of gray whales in Mexico, Emily and I spent six months living, fishing, and talking with the residents of Magdalena Bay. Occasionally a fisherman would drop us off on one of the islands. There I would spend a few days surfing razor-sharp reefs by myself while Emily observed the harvest of abalone and the slaughter of sea turtles firsthand.

To the outsider, Magdalena Bay's ecological and cultural richness is overwhelming. Unlocking the area's secrets requires understanding the lifeways of the people who inhabit it.

Peeking into the Past

The town of La Poza Grande sits at the extreme northern edge of the esteros and mangroves of the bay. The town exists because of the tenacity and determination of Agostino Olivas, one of the oldest fishermen in the region. Emily and I found the ninety-five-year-old Agostino one afternoon, sitting on a bench in the patio of his whitewashed adobe house. With his smooth, dark skin, he didn't look a day over seventy.

In 1904, at the age of eight, Agostino made his first visit to Magdalena Bay with his father, John Oliver, a Scots whaler who had washed ashore in the late nineteenth century. Sixteen years later, when Agostino moved to Magdalena Bay with his family from a mountain ranch, there were few other fishermen and no towns. With abundant sea life, the Olivas family would not starve. They might, however, die of thirst. Agostino was lucky and discovered water. The name of the town he founded, La Poza Grande, means the "Big Well."

His many adventures included walking miles to Scammon's Lagoon at the age of fourteen with his father and two American treasure seekers. "I cannot discuss it; I suffered too much," he said. After fighting in the Mexican Revolution, Agostino moved his family to Magdalena Bay. He has been there ever since.

Despite an ample supply of food, being a fisherman was never easy. *Pangas*, or skiffs, were made by hand, from wood dropped off by schooners or scavenged from shipwrecks. Agostino used oars and sails to navigate the bay. He never ventured into the open ocean with his small panga. Why risk death? There was plenty of sea life inside the bay. Harpooning turtles and sharks was hard. Selling them was nearly impossible. The nearest market was two days inland by burro. A load of sea turtles brought a few pesos, enough for some flour and sugar.

Agostino's daughter Ramona remembers that there was never much money, but there was always enough food. One visit from a friend initiated a fiesta. "We ate every type of *caguama* [sea turtle] dish you can imagine. It was wonderful," she said.

For Agostino, the life of a fisherman was a practical solution to an economic problem. He could have remained inland and worked for a pittance, but he preferred to fish. Despite his assertion that fishing was just a job, Agostino is proud of his fishing cooperative. He is happy that his sons and grandsons are also fishermen. When I asked him if he was a good fisherman, Agostino smiled and said, "They say I was."

As Emily and I listened to Agostino in his garden, family members stopped in to say hello. By the time we left, over nineteen had gathered. I asked if it was unusual for so many people to visit. His daughter Nena laughed and said, "We visit twice a day, every day of the week."

A year after I met Agostino, he passed away in his small adobe house. Friends and family from throughout the Baja California peninsula gathered around his deathbed. A few days before he died, he visited Ramona in the fishing village of Puerto Adolfo Lopez Mateos. Ramona later told me with tears in her eyes, "Every day when the *muchachos* would come in from fishing, he'd slowly walk over to the beach and watch them bring in the day's catch. They reminded him of his sons."

Life among the Mangroves

Marcial Canchola lives in El Cayuco, a small fish camp across from the peaks of Isla Margarita at the southern end of the bay. Upon our arrival, Marcial popped his head out of an opening in his sturdy palapa and invited Emily and me in for a cup of coffee. Inside we found Marcial preparing coffee next to his stove, made from an empty metal barrel fueled by dried cactus and mesquite.

A lifelong fisherman, Marcial was born on Tres Marias Island. He was a wiry and handsome man who attributed his good health to the many oysters he eats after weekend *borracheras* (drunken binges). Over coffee and a few rounds of Pacifico beer, he invited us to accompany him the next morning on a fishing trip.

Marcial and his assistant, Fermín, took us out in a panga early in the morning. As we turned into a small inlet, they kept their eyes on the pelicans that followed us. There were few fish in evidence, for the tide was too high for them. We turned into a tiny opening in the mangroves to wait for low tide. The pelicans remained close by.

On the beach, Marcial and Fermín pointed out useful plants. *Galletilla* is a tiny plant that grows in the sand. When boiled in water, it reduces the pain of a stingray barb. Fermín broke the stem of a *candelilla* plant and rubbed its milky juice over his arm. The juice heals sunburn, chapped lips, and other skin ailments. *Pitaya agria*, a sprawling, multibranched cactus, was everywhere. Its tasty red fruit ripens in the late summer and early fall.

Marcial decided it was time to fish. Fermín stood in the prow looking for schools of mullet. Marcial yelled at Fermín to get the nets ready and headed off a school of fish by steering the boat in a circular motion. Fermín rapidly threw out the net. Marcial completed the circle and stopped the engine. They remained silent while we pulled in the net. The fish they caught would not even pay for gas. Marcial turned the boat around, and we headed home.

Pointing out to the open expanse of Magdalena Bay, Marcial said, "I will never starve to death, but I might die of thirst." Because his car had broken down, Marcial relied on others to bring the water he and his goats needed. On occasion when he required supplies, the sixty-year-old Marcial hiked fifteen miles to the nearest town.

Upon our return, we found Marcial's brother, Silvestre, who had arrived from San Blas. While we were out fishing, Silvestre caught a few kilos of shrimp with a throw net and cooked them up. Marcial placed the shrimp on a table under the palo verde tree in the center of his yard. "I want the fishermen *al otro lado*"—meaning "the other side," that is, in the United States—"to know how we live. To understand our lives. To know what we do," he said.

The Island

The islands that protect Magdalena Bay from the open ocean are only a few miles from the desert shore. Yet they are a world apart. Miles of sand dunes stretch forth without a trace of footsteps. Coyotes search the beaches for dead sea turtles. Bones of whales long dead litter the beaches. Shipwrecks provide refuge for pelicans, cormorants, and blue herons.

The people of the mangroves tell stories of treasure left on the islands by English pirates such as Sir Francis Drake and Sir Thomas Cavendish. The Spanish caught their first glimpse of Magdalena Bay and its mangroves in 1539 but were driven off by Indian attacks. Others searched for treasure in the form of gold, pearls, sea turtles, and whale oil. Most of them were unsuccessful. The remains of their failed settlements and schemes dot the islands. They left a path of destruction in their wake. At the beginning of the twentieth century, most of the gray whales had been slaughtered. American companies were taking thousands of sea turtles a year from the lagoons of Baja California, including Magdalena Bay.

Franciscillo (I never asked him his last name) makes the trip from Puerto Adolfo Lopez Mateos to the fish camp on Magdalena Island near Cabo San Lázaro three times a week. It is a hard journey. Supplies are loaded on a panga that navigates the channel to a blue Ford flatbed truck sitting among the dunes of the island. Two to three boat trips are required to load up the cans of water, ice, food, and people who make the half-day journey across the island to reach the fish camp deep inside the mangroves.

Franciscillo gruffly accepted my request to have Emily and me join him on his island journey. After the skiff was loaded with about seven hundred pounds of ice and our supplies, eight fishermen joined us as we made our way across the channel. In the middle of the channel, the engine stopped. Nobody showed much concern. A large bottle of Pacifico beer was passed around while the driver tinkered with the outboard engine. As we finished the bottle, the outboard kicked in, and we continued the crossing.

After we transferred ice and our gear to the truck, someone noticed that the rear tire was low. We took turns pumping the tire with a hand pump.

Lurching across the dunes to the beach caused the truck's U-joint to give out. Franciscillo and the fishermen returned to Puerto Adolfo Lopez Mateos to find a replacement part. Emily and I were left alone with Solovino, an angry Siamese cat that had been tied up in a flour sack during the boat crossing.

Six hours later everyone returned. After walking two miles across the dunes and flagging down a panga to cross the bay, they hitched to Ciudad Insurgentes, the nearest town, to find a replacement part. Although Franciscillo denied that his nonstop schedule was too demanding, his bloodshot eyes proved that he needed a break and to stop drinking. Franciscillo drove down the deserted beach as he nursed a Pacifico between his legs. "Something goes wrong every day, six days a week," he said.

After driving more than twenty miles north on the deserted beach to the San Lázaro fish camp, we left the shoreline. Franciscillo downshifted as we headed up and over a hill and passed a small mangrove lagoon. The fishermen crossed themselves as we descended and passed a shrine built into the side of a cliff. Salt water ate away the truck brakes years ago. No one wanted to be left behind there.

Making a living on the islands and among the mangroves is grueling. The adversity that the people of Magdalena Bay face every day was hard for me to comprehend. I asked Francisco Javier, who shares an island palapa with his cousin, Cosme, and whose grandfathers and great-uncles first settled the bay in the 1920s, why he fished. Wouldn't he rather move to the city and work in a bank?

"My grandfather was a fisherman," Francisco replied. "My father is a fisherman. Everyone in my family is a fisherman. That's what we do. Working in a bank would be more secure. Sometimes we spend all our money on gasoline and we catch nothing. Other times we make a lot of money. I didn't have much choice."

After we arrived at the San Lázaro fish camp set at the edge of the mangrove lagoon, Emily made arrangements to be picked up the next day so she could observe the abalone harvest. I loaded our gear in Francisco's panga. An hour later, he dropped us off at a tiny cove at Cabo San Lázaro. We were all alone.

After setting up our wobbly dome tent held together with duct tape and bungee cords, I paddled out to surf a nearby reef. I immediately snagged the third wave of a shoulder-high set. An open wall followed the tight drop. A flat spot allowed time for a clean cutback. I set up for the inside, kicking out in time to avoid a large rock. My hands scraped the bottom as I paddled back outside.

As the sun set over the cinder cone peak behind our camp, a sea lion popped its head up next to me. I caught a few more waves and paddled in. The only locals were the sea lions bobbing around the point, sea turtles that munch on eelgrass on the inside coves, and *duendes*, mischief-loving goblins that the people of the mangroves swear live in caves on the island. Coyote eyes flashed in the light of our campfire as we zipped up the tent to go to sleep. The duendes left us alone.

The next morning the Camacho cousins, Martín and Calilo, arrived to take Emily fishing. Martín with his huge belly and scraggly two-day beard looked like a linebacker for the Raiders. As Emily boarded the skiff, Calilo laughed and said, "We told Martín we were tired of giving him all our food and trying to fit two wet suits together so he could dive. It is cheaper for all of us if he just drives the boat."

After the skiff departed, I paddled out to surf the Garambullero, an amphitheater cove up the beach from the reef I surfed the day before. At low tide, an A-frame bowl throws out in front of a rock shelf right outside the cove.

There was no time for a bottom turn as I caught a wave and drove high and fast in front of rocks only yards away. With inches to spare, I passed through, floated down with the white water, and cruised through the inside section that peels off into a crystal-clear wall.

As I kicked out, I looked up into the garambullo cactus on the cliff above the cove. The duendes were out there watching. They controlled the lineup at Cabo San Lázaro. No matter how well I thought I had the takeoff wired, the duendes changed the configuration of the rocks every time. Duendes teach gringo surfers a lesson in humility that the people of the mangroves have long since learned.

Beyond the Present

Humberto "Diablo" Victoria, a stocky, friendly fisherman with a big laugh, took me out early one morning to see the mangrove island in the middle of the gray whale calving area. Located about six miles south of Puerto Adolfo Lopez Mateos, the largest town in the northern portion of the bay, the island is where hundreds of blue herons and cormorants make their home. This area of narrow channels and dense islands is dominated by the presence of tall, thick mangroves.

The tide was high and the sky overcast. A fog bank hung above the water. We passed a gray whale calf poking its head out of the water around the pier adjacent to the fish cannery at the edge of town. The whale looked almost white in the fog.

Diablo had spent the previous three months working as a whale-watching guide. He said, "The gray whales are leaving. The season is almost over. Time to get the nets ready and go fishing."

As Diablo and I rounded a bend in the channel, a forty-five-foot gray whale leapt into the air. The noise of the splash caused by its body crashing into the water was absorbed by the fog and sand dunes along the shore. Diablo smiled as we passed the breaching whale. Watching until the fog obscured the cetacean, Diablo accelerated as we continued southward. The mangroves were waiting.

3

How Saving Whales Advances Democracy

In 1995 I notified Homero Aridjis, Mexico's leading environmentalist and a well-respected novelist and poet, about the proposed San Ignacio Lagoon salt project. We have collaborated ever since. Rather than frame this essay (which we published in the Los Angeles Times) purely around environmental issues, we argued that the activists fighting the project were involved in the struggle for a more democratic Mexico.

The most consequential political campaigns for the future of Mexico were not those being orchestrated by the dinosaurs of the then long-dominant Institutional Revolutionary Party (PRI) or by members of the opposition parties. Rather, the campaign with the greatest implication for democracy in Mexico was the one being waged over the gray whale—a marine mammal that spends each winter in the secluded Pacific lagoons of Baja California.

Since 1995, environmental groups had attempted to prevent Exportadora de Sal, a company jointly owned by the Mexican government (51 percent) and the Mitsubishi Corporation of Japan (49 percent), from building the world's largest salt production facility on the shoreline of San Ignacio Lagoon, the last undeveloped gray whale refuge on Earth. The lagoon is the cultural and ecological heart of the 6.2-million-acre Vizcaino Biosphere Reserve, the largest protected area in Mexico and Latin America.

The industrial salt facility would have destroyed more than 500,000 acres inside the reserve—an area larger than Rocky Mountain National Park and more than twice the size of the lagoon. Herminio Blanco, the powerful chief of Mexico's Ministry of Commerce and Industry, and Baja California Sur governor Leonel Cota championed the project.

The first-ever primary to pick the PRI's presidential candidate made very few changes to a political system dominated by the "Revolutionary Family." In contrast, the battle over San Ignacio Lagoon and its gray whales would determine whether Mexico evolved into a nation that permitted private citizens and nonaligned organizations to participate in national policy and local economic development debates.

The controversy over the salt project became so heated that Environment Minister Julia Carabias lashed out at environmentalists for a campaign she said did a "disservice" to Mexico by assaulting its sovereignty. That the Mexican government feigned surprise at opposition to the salt project and the spirited defense of the gray whale by conservationists was astonishing. For years, the federal government had made the gray whale an animal superstar. In 1994, the Ministry of Fisheries aired public service commercials nationally that displayed frolicking gray whales with a message that flashed, "In Mexico, we protect you."

Ironically, former president Luis Echeverría had made San Ignacio Lagoon a wildlife refuge in 1972 to protect it from the foreign-financed development that Exportadora de Sal proposed. Gray whale conservation in Mexico was partly a reaction to the legacy of American whalers hunting the mammal to near extinction in the nineteenth century. Because of this history, Echeverría declared that protecting such coastal areas was "an example of the long and difficult fight to ensure sovereignty over natural resources."[4]

What the gray whale campaign truly demonstrated, however, was the limited value of multiparty elections when the PRI includes opposition politicians who are still dependent on federal funds to govern. When Governor Cota—a former member of the PRI who switched his affiliation to the Revolutionary Democratic Party (PRD) for political expediency—took office in the spring of 1999, he immediately assumed control of the pro-salt project campaign. That effort had been initiated by his predecessor, Guillermo Mercado, a member of the PRI, who governed the state into near bankruptcy and was arrested for diverting a reported $55 million in public funds.

Despite the obstacles that the PRI placed on open political participation in Mexico, fishermen and whale-watching guides from San Ignacio Lagoon were eloquent opponents of the project. Their participation in the gray whale campaign was a sign that local people felt more empowered to question the dictates of the ruling party.

In a letter to President Ernesto Zedillo, Jorge Peon (a lagoon fishing cooperative member) asked, "Do you expect that when plans are announced to build an industrial project that will take millions of gallons of water out of our lagoon, that we will hold a party and welcome the project even though we know it will destroy the resources we depend on?"[5]

The fishermen and conservationists involved in the gray whale campaign were the real key to a more open and pluralistic political system in Mexico. A real and vibrant democracy will exist in Mexico only when independent groups are allowed to emerge from the shadows of the central government.

Mexican president Ernesto Zedillo cancelled the salt project on March 2, 2000.

4

Protecting Mexico's Natural Heritage

Soon after his inauguration, Mexican president Vicente Fox announced plans to build the Escalera Nautica marina project almost exactly a year after the cancellation of the Mitsubishi salt project. The proposed yacht harbor project resulted in a wave of land speculation in some of Baja California's most remote coastal areas. Homero Aridjis and I wrote this editorial in the San Diego Union-Tribune *after learning of the development scheme.*

The blue waters of Bahía de los Angeles, on Mexico's Baja California peninsula, confirm Jacques Cousteau's statement that the Sea of Cortez is the world's aquarium. Thousands of dolphins chase millions of sardines. Sea lions breed on islands among plants, mammals, and reptiles that exist nowhere else on Earth. During summer and fall, whale sharks arrive to feed on plankton.

Bahía de los Angeles is unique. If President Vicente Fox and John McCarthy of Mexico's National Tourism Fund (FONATUR) had their way, the natural beauty and marine wildlife of the bay would have disappeared. Whale sharks would have been replaced by an 1,800-slip yacht marina. Jet skis would have stopped the dolphin's underwater ballet. A marine area considered by scientists and conservation groups to be among the most biologically important on earth might have been lost forever.

The proposed yacht marina resort with hotels and a golf course planned for Bahía de los Angeles—an area that under Mexican law should be off-limits for development—was one of twenty-six tourist projects planned for Mexico's Sea of Cortez and the Baja California peninsula, despite the potentially significant impacts to one of North America's most sensitive marine areas. The $1.6 billion chain of marinas and tourist resorts, known as the "Nautical Ladder," threatened some of the world's most visually stunning and ecologically significant wildlife reserves: the Upper Gulf Biosphere Reserve, Loreto Bay National Park,

Sea of Cortez Islands Wildlife Refuge, Los Cirios Wildlife Conservation Area, and the Vizcaino Biosphere Reserve.

These five sites had been targeted for development without consultation with the dedicated specialists responsible for managing these great marine, island, and coastal wildlife hot spots. The planners certainly did not consult the fishermen who depend on the natural resources of these areas to feed their families.

During Fox's first visit to the United States as Mexico's first democratically elected leader, he highlighted his government's commitment to democracy, free trade, and immigration reform. However, in the aftermath of the terrorist attacks on the United States, the U.S. Congress abandoned immigration reform, the centerpiece of Fox's economic development policy. The Fox administration was left instead with the Nautical Ladder.

Unfortunately, government-financed development projects, classic white elephants, litter the Baja California peninsula. Deserted government trailer parks, roadside cafeterias, and gas stations dot the Transpeninsular Highway. Their presence highlights the inability of bureaucrats in Mexico City to plan successful projects.

The Nautical Ladder was a clever publicly financed land grab that promised to enrich a small cadre of public officials and a select group of private investors. The support by the Fox administration for the Nautical Ladder sadly exposed the tradition of authoritarian and antidemocratic decision making among presidents in Mexico that was the hallmark of the seventy-one-year rule by the Institutional Revolutionary Party.

A map of the Nautical Ladder project published by FONATUR showed that one marina would be built in exactly the same location, in Punta Abreojos (just north of San Ignacio Lagoon and in the path of a gray whale migration corridor), where a mile-long concrete pier associated with the Mitsubishi salt project had been planned. The marina site was located within the Vizcaino Biosphere Reserve.

During a visit to Bahía de los Angeles, FONATUR's John McCarthy derided local fishermen who publicly argued that the marina project would destroy the local ecotourism and sport fishing industries—the main source of jobs in the town. Because Bahía de los Angeles barely has enough water for the town's existing eight hundred residents, it was hard to believe that water would have magically appeared for the 1,200 hotel rooms planned for a region with little rainfall.

The future of Baja California lies not in the white elephants planned by FONATUR that would end up unfinished and rotting under the desert

The failed Nautical Ladder marina at Santa Rosalillita, Baja California.

sun. Economic development and progress must be through investment in ecotourism, sustainable fishing, and biodiversity conservation. These activities will create more opportunities for rural communities in Baja California than wasting public funds on tourist megaprojects that are relics of Mexico's corrupt past.

Mexico's Ministry of Tourism finally cancelled the Nautical Ladder project in 2007. Transpeninsular Highway road signs and an abandoned marina in the Pacific coast village of Santa Rosalillita are all that remain of the scheme.

5

Life for the Sea

Fishermen and Surfers in Baja California

During our effort to stop the black market sea turtle trade in Baja California, my Wildcoast colleagues and I assisted fishermen from Magdalena Bay, San Ignacio Lagoon, and Punta Abreojos in their effort to stop poaching. These fishermen became our biggest allies in supporting conservation programs to protect the coast and fishing resources they depend on for their livelihoods.

When Mitsubishi announced plans to overrun the fishing village of Punta Abreojos (located just north of San Ignacio Lagoon) with a concrete pier for an industrial salt harvesting operation, Isidro Arce, a fisherman, fought the project. It was not an easy task for Isidro, whose grandfather had helped found Punta Abreojos—especially because Mitsubishi, one of the world's largest corporations, was claiming that the salt project would provide jobs for his neighbors.

"Some people in town wanted the *salinera*, but I didn't," Isidro said to me one day at his parents' house a couple blocks from the beach.

Isidro is six feet tall, with the burly build that comes from years of hauling up lobster traps and fishing nets. After the salt project was cancelled, Isidro focused on halting nightly raids by poachers that threatened 250 fishing cooperative jobs and $5 million in annual revenues from the lucrative international trade in lobster and abalone.

Compared to the other fishing villages throughout the Baja California Peninsula, Punta Abreojos is a model of fisheries conservation and management. The fishing cooperative there has successfully managed its lobster and abalone fisheries for fifty years. Due to the exclusive control they have over their fishing territory through a government-granted concession, Abreojos fishermen have an incentive to manage local fisheries for the long term. That concession grants the Punta Abreojos cooperative the right to ban outsiders fishing there.

The Catholic Church, baseball, and the fishing cooperative anchor Punta Abreojos. Many of the kids who surf give up the sport once they become members of the fishing cooperative. Fishermen come in from a morning *marea* and return home to change out of their foul-weather gear into pressed polo shirts and pants. Surfing does not fit into the community's cloistered view of responsible adulthood.

After fellow *cooperativistas* from La Bocana, a fishing village to the north, exchanged gunfire with poachers, killing two of them, Isidro did not shed any tears. When corrupt government officials released poachers caught by the Abreojos Cooperative, co-op members conducted a five-day blockade of Highway 1 to protest the lax treatment of Baja's worst seafood thieves. The effort paid off. Military detachments and state police began assisting the effort by local cooperatives to halt poachers. But the fight against poachers is an ongoing battle.

But for Isidro the effort to stop poaching also means changing local attitudes in Punta Abreojos about killing federally protected species such as sea turtles, once a plentiful part of the local diet and culture. One day a few of the town's senior residents asked Isidro if they could kill a sea turtle to celebrate the town's patron saint. Isidro said, "I don't think the Catholic Church sanctions killing endangered species for religious ceremonies."

San Ignacio Lagoon

Francisco "Pachico" Mayoral lives in the La Laguna fish camp on the shore of San Ignacio Lagoon. The first fisherman to come in contact with a friendly gray whale, Pachico has assisted many of the scientists who studied gray whales in San Ignacio Lagoon. His four sons manage two family-owned eco-camps during the whale-watching season.

I shuttled back and forth between San Ignacio Lagoon and Punta Abreojos with my Wildcoast colleague Wallace "J." Nichols. The lagoon is a major center for the black market trade in sea turtles and became a major focus of our work to protect the marine reptiles from the predations of poachers.

One day while J. drove his 1971 International on the sixty-mile rutted dirt road to Punta Abreojos, the rear axle fell off. After waiting more than twenty hours for a tow truck to arrive, he arrived in San Ignacio and met Francisco "Gordo" (Fatso) Fischer, whose belly fits his nickname.

Gordo appeared intrigued by J.'s graduate research on sea turtles. He offered to give J. a lift to San Ignacio Lagoon to find some turtles. When the gringo biologist showed up at the lagoon asking for information on sea turtles accompanied by Mexico's most notorious poacher, salty fishermen who grew up drinking sea turtle blood swore they'd never seen one before.

According to Antonio Aguilar, a San Ignacio Lagoon fisherman, "After J. left with Gordo, a detachment of soldiers with machine guns came to the house looking for the gringo trying to buy sea turtles." Gordo later spent time in jail again after he was caught with a truckload of sea turtles near Rancho San Angel.

I ran into Gordo in San Ignacio Lagoon after he was released from jail. "I was in jail for a while," he said sadly. "I'm fishing now. I'm not involved in that other stuff anymore."

Antonio was later criticized for hiring Gordo to help him harvest fan scallops. "It is better to have Gordo where I can see him," Antonio told me over a plate of scallop ceviche. "We don't want to have him out of work and have to go back to poaching sea turtles. I keep tabs on him here."

Antonio's wife, Maria Luisa, is one of the best cooks in Baja. *Arroz con codorñiz* (rice with quail) and *ceviche de pulpo* (octopus ceviche) are two of my favorite dishes. Although Maria Luisa loves serving *caguama*, or sea turtle, she proudly said, "None of my children like to eat it anymore."

On a trip to Antonio's house, I found it a little intimidating to be stopped and searched by plainclothes *judiciales* (state police) with pistols sticking out of the back of their pants. On the lookout for poachers, they backed off when I said that I was friends with Isidro Arce and Antonio (who was the uncle of one of the policemen).

Unhappy with police efforts to halt the poachers who use San Ignacio Lagoon as a staging ground for their night raids on Punta Abreojos, Isidro said, "I want to get a naval base built in the lagoon. We need greater firepower there."

Magdalena Bay

Miguel Lizarraga is a quiet and reserved fisherman who lives in the Magdalena Bay fishing town of Puerto San Carlos. He led local efforts to stop the *piratas* (poachers) who thrive in Magdalena Bay.

One day, after Miguel confiscated eight illegal sea turtle nets from Estero Banderitas, he led a detachment of marines to pangas belonging to Chino Cazares, a poacher with an enormous beer belly. Chino had just returned from a night raid on local scallop beds. Enraged, Chino took a swing at Miguel. After ducking Chino's meaty fist, Miguel punched Chino.

Soon after, the Fisheries Agency accused Miguel's cooperative of being too "*ecologista*" and denied its members permits to harvest fan scallops (which they protected from poachers) for six months. Miguel and his fellow cooperativistas blockaded the main highway into Puerto San Carlos. Soon after, they received their permits (blockading highways is a common form of protest in Mexico).

For one of Miguel's friends, Adan Hernandez, stopping poachers is easy. If he spots a sea turtle in a panga, he picks it up and throws it back into the bay.

Semana Santa, or Easter Week, is the most popular time to eat sea turtle in Baja. Many Baja California peninsula residents mistakenly believe that a sea turtle is a fish rather than a reptile and therefore appropriate to eat during Lent. During one Semana Santa, Adan and Miguel visited scores of families from all over Baja California Sur camping on the shoreline of Magdalena Bay to warn them not to kill turtles. Adan and Miguel hauled out three sea turtle nets in front of the owners, who watched silently from shore.

On the way down to Magdalena Bay, I stopped to surf second-point San Juanico. Out in the lineup I mentioned to a forty-something American padding back out to the point with me that a planned marina could kill the waves we were enjoying. "Oh, well, that's progress," he replied.

Adan viewed the issue a little differently. "Fishermen don't want to work as janitors and waiters," he said. Miguel, Adan, and Isidro want to continue their life in the sea. They just want to protect their fishing grounds and villages from poachers and ill-conceived development schemes.

Once after attending an environmental conference in Malibu with Isidro, I drove him to Tijuana so he could catch a bus back to Punta Abreojos. I asked him whether he would prefer living in Los Angeles over Punta Abreojos. After quickly surveying the urban sprawl surrounding Interstate 405, he replied, "Why would I ever want to leave Punta Abreojos? We don't lock our doors. We make good money. I like my town the way it is. We're lucky."

6

The Baja California Land Rush

A global economy awash in cash caused a frontierlike land rush in the Baja California peninsula from 2000 to 2008. The most outlandish resort and industrial development projects sprouted up. Some conservationists raced to stop some of the more environmentally damaging projects. Others focused their efforts on preserving some of the peninsula's most biologically significant coastal areas, such as San Ignacio Lagoon.

Bajamar, a gated golf and resort coastal community about thirty-five miles south of the U.S.–Mexico border, is the type of development that environmentalists love to hate. The twenty-seven-hole golf course, billed as "Pebble Beach South of the Border," is built on a coastal bluff surrounded by pristine coastal sage scrub, with some of the finest ocean views north of Ensenada. More than 360 Spanish Colonial–style homes surround the golf course. Guests and residents are primarily from the United States.

A closer look reveals that nature is not dead at Bajamar. Large swaths of native scrub remain within its 650-acre grounds, and agaves (century plants) grow here and there. Red-tailed hawks on the lookout for prey patrol the fairways. Bajamar's developers worked with a team of conservation biologists from the Center for Scientific Research and Higher Education of Ensenada to preserve open space within the compound and also the coastal sage around it.

Despite these efforts to balance profits and the environment, what happens outside the resort's boundaries is beyond Bajamar's control. Nor does any zoning or coastal plan protect against incompatible land uses. In 2005, Sempra Energy began building a $700 million liquefied natural gas (LNG) terminal just south of Bajamar, at a facility called Costa Azul. President Felipe Calderon inaugurated the plant in the fall of 2008. The facility did not receive its first natural gas shipment until August 2009.[6] Bill Powers, who contested the Costa Azul project, told me, "The area developed by Sempra Energy was either completely undeveloped or [has]

Harry's surf spot in Baja California, which was destroyed as a result of the Sempra Energy LNG plant.

low-impact development. The construction of a huge industrial facility at the site changed it from a rural windswept coast to one of the two biggest industrial facilities on Baja's coast."

The Baja Boom

From 2000 to 2008, quiet seaside villages and fishing settlements along the peninsula's Pacific coastline were transformed into the Wild West of Mexico. Rosarito Beach and other boomtowns are now filled with high-rise Cancun-style condo fortresses, gaudy narco-deco-styled spring-break hotels, and opulent mansions. But outside the party zones can be found more and more industrial development, buttressed by shantytowns where raw sewage and garbage flow freely into the ocean.

The exorbitant cost of coastal housing in Southern California, combined with the opening of lands in Baja California that were previously locked out of development by legal constraints, created a land rush—the "Baja Boom." The natural coastal landscape was carved up for residential and vacation developments at a frenzied pace.

Investing in real estate has always been a risky business in Mexico. Investors who purchase a home site at a high-end, well-planned golf resort might one day learn that their neighbor will be an industrial facility that communities in California such as Long Beach, Malibu, Oxnard, and Ventura fought to keep out of their backyards.

Throughout much of the Baja California peninsula, coastal land is owned by ejidos. A few of these rank among the largest in Mexico, comprising more than a million acres, with up to fifty miles of undeveloped shoreline graced by picturesque beaches and bays, as well as some of North America's most pristine wetlands.

Until 1992, foreigners could not legally own land in Mexico, and ejido land could not be sold. Then, under former president Carlos Salinas de Gortari, Article 27 of the Constitution was amended to facilitate the modernization of agriculture. The redistribution of land through governmental expropriation was prohibited; subdivided communal lands can now be rented and, in some instances, sold to other farmers or multinational corporations. Corporations, both domestic and foreign, can now own coastal land. This was a significant repudiation of the Mexican Revolution and a defining moment in Mexico's land use policy.[7]

Ejido members began to privatize collective lands—and then sell lots on the open market. However, because Mexican federal agricultural officials often took up to a decade to survey and title *ejidal* lands throughout the Baja California peninsula, many have come on the market only in the past few years. Many ejidatarios tend to be land rich and cash poor, so when developers offer them quick cash for their acreage, many jump at the chance to bring in income. The buyers very often represent land speculators and developer syndicates. The result is the potential destruction of many of the Baja California peninsula's most scenic and ecologically significant natural sites, especially along the coast.

Post-NAFTA Deals

Contributing to the boom is the North American Free Trade Agreement (NAFTA) of 1994, which eased restrictions on transborder commerce. Some of the world's largest corporations began looking at Baja California as a possible location for industrial projects—especially those that cannot easily be built north of the border because they are considered hazardous or potentially polluting. The fact that coastal real estate is much cheaper in Mexico than in the United States was definitely a plus. Areas that have

Development at Loreto Bay in Baja California Sur.

been targeted for development include some of the finest remaining examples of coastal desert and coastal sage scrub ecosystems left on earth.

Eighty miles south of Ensenada, at Punta Colonet, a network of Mexican and Asian investors is planning to build a new 27,000-acre megaport industrial complex, complete with a new city for 250,000 residents. The proposed facility is designed to compete with the ports of Long Beach and Los Angeles. Farther south, several large development projects have been proposed for the now tranquil embayment of Bahía Concepción, which contains white sand beaches, islands, and some of the most ecologically sensitive coastal mangrove wetlands in the Sea of Cortez. Loreto and the East Cape have already been transformed by large-scale tourism development. Aware that time is running out for Baja's coastline, a network of Mexican and American conservationists joined together to put the brakes on the anything-goes development and to save at least some of Baja's most pristine coastal areas.

The focal point of the current Baja Boom is the sixty-mile stretch of coastline between Tijuana and Ensenada. Until the 1990s, this area was characterized primarily by small U.S.-expatriate settlements and the then-small tourist town of Rosarito Beach, connected by a four-lane toll road.

Now "For Sale" signs dot the edges of the coastal highway. The steel frames of abandoned high-rise condos loom beside ramshackle coastal shantytowns.

Tijuana is expanding southward and now extends to the edge of Rosarito Beach—miles from the border. So great is the local demand for housing in Tijuana that new developments and *colonias* are spilling out onto the coastal plain just north and east of Rosarito and even beyond the barren brown-colored mountains to the east.

One of the biggest concerns that residents have is the lack of wastewater infrastructure adequate to meet the needs of existing and proposed development. Existing sewage pump stations break down continually because of power outages and leaks. Half of Tijuana's estimated population of two million lives in colonias without wastewater treatment, so sewage is often dumped directly onto the beach—even at the upscale Playas de Tijuana just south of the U.S.–Mexico border.[8] Other colonias are served by septic systems, with hulking trucks pumping up the sludge and, often, emptying their loads directly into arroyos that lead to the beach.

A mere six miles south of the U.S.–Mexico border, up to 30 million gallons of treated and untreated (50-50) sewage are dumped daily onto the beach at Punta Banderas, located alongside a golf resort and just south of the site of the now cancelled Trump Ocean Resort Baja. The Trump Baja Web site once displayed a seaside swimming pool adjacent to rocky cliffs proclaiming that its "oceanfront living" would appeal to "senses that will stir your soul." Irongate Development, the company that bought the rights to use the Trump name in Baja, allegedly sold more than $122 million of the condo-hotel residences at a sales event in San Diego in December 2006.[9] The cancellation of the project resulted in a plethora of lawsuits by investors and Donald Trump against Irongate.

In 2006, Baja California officials estimated that more than twenty-four large projects with over 2,800 residential units were planned in the area between Tijuana and Ensenada, including more than a dozen condo towers.[10] A new four-lane highway, Boulevard 2000, now connects eastern Tijuana to the seaside community of Popotla, just south of Rosarito Beach. It runs mostly through undeveloped and sparsely inhabited chaparral ranchland.

Sewage to the Beach

In building the new highway, Baja California officials seem to have anticipated the development boom that has doubled the size of Tijuana and

A river of sewage at Punta Banderas south of Tijuana.

Rosarito Beach in the past decade. How odd, therefore, that they failed to invest in the construction of appropriate wastewater treatment plants for the existing residents of the region who lack basic services.

In the small beachside community of Campo Torres, north of Rosarito, forty-eight-year-old Mark Padilla (who has been a part-time resident for thirty-four years) documented a stream of sewage that empties onto the beach next to his house, courtesy of the San Marino housing development across the toll road. His landlord gave permission to the developer to dump the sewage into an arroyo on her property. "I just can't believe that it is legal," Padilla told me.

Matt Hoffower, a thirty-three-year-old surfer, echoed Padilla. He recently moved back to San Diego after living in Rosarito Beach with his wife and son while working as a real estate agent. "Living in Baja is hard," he said. "The arroyos are horrible and filled with trash." Hoffower smiled as he said, "I used to tell the agents I worked with, 'You see how the ocean is glassy? That's from the sewage in the water. That isn't natural.' They didn't want to believe me. I couldn't justify selling property with conditions like that."

The real estate boom in northern Baja California is a vivid lesson for conservationists concerned with preserving undeveloped coastal areas south of Ensenada. Because they are remote, and hours by car from the nearest paved road, many wild areas in Baja California had, until recently, been considered undevelopable. For example, the uncrowded point surf and excellent fishing found in Punta Abreojos attracts mostly surfers and fishermen. Now the state of Baja California Sur has proposed a cruise ship terminal there.

For Fernando Ochoa, an attorney who directs the Northwest Environmental Law Center in Ensenada (one of only two nonprofit environmental law firms in Mexico), the number of development projects in Baja is "overwhelming." Ochoa, who is originally from Mexico City, said, "The total budget for conservation of the Mexican government and NGOs is literally millions of times less than what is destined for development. There are not enough people working in the conservation field compared to the development field."

Nevertheless, Ochoa successfully blocked efforts by FONATUR to build a marina in a wetland just north of Bahía de los Angeles. He prevailed on behalf of local fishermen and community residents who use the wetland for fishing and recreation. After that victory, Ochoa switched his focus to blocking the cruise ship terminal in Punta Abreojos, with the help of Mexico's Group of 100, the Natural Resources Defense Council (NRDC), and Wildcoast.

"We want to see development that complies with Mexican laws so there is sustainable development, healthy communities, and projects that are appropriate for the natural environment where they are proposed," said Ochoa. "Punta Abreojos is not an appropriate location for a cruise ship terminal. Since the community has an economy based on fishing, they need projects that correspond to the needs of the community."

Ochoa believes that working with local landowners to make conservation an economic option is the best way to balance preservation with economic development. "Poverty is a cultural and social problem in Mexico," he said. "If poor people who own nothing but their land sell out to a speculator for a low price, they will either become destitute where they live or they will have to migrate to a city to work." What are needed are financial incentives for rural landowners to adopt conservation measures on their properties.

In San Ignacio Lagoon, the strategy of land conservation combined with sustainable development has proved effective. About five hundred local residents make their living from fishing and working in the whale-watching industry.

In 2001, Exportadora de Sal renewed its concession to harvest salt from the lagoon, and rumors spread that the company planned to renew the large-scale salt project. In response, local landowners joined forces in 2003 with NRDC, Pronatura Noroeste, Wildcoast, and the International Community Foundation to form the Laguna San Ignacio Conservation Alliance. The purpose of the alliance was to establish a conservation agreement with the Ejido Luis Echeverría, which owns 140,000 acres of the lagoon's southern shore. The alliance also planned to conserve 860,000 additional acres of lagoon habitat and help support local livelihoods.[11]

The result was a pioneering deal between the alliance and the Ejido Luis Echeverría to protect all of the land within its boundaries. The area included much of the southern portion of the lagoon's watershed. In return, the alliance established a $725,000 trust fund for the ejido and $500,000 in direct payments to its forty-four members.[12] Alliance members, including Wildcoast, are now negotiating another deal with a neighboring ejido to conserve 18,000 acres.

The challenge for conservationists and residents of coastal Baja California will be finding a balance between the desire for progress and growth that drives the modern economy of Mexico and the concern for preserving coastal habitats that exist nowhere else on earth. Raúl López, the president of Ejido Luis Echeverría, helped broker the deal to preserve San Ignacio Lagoon and earns his living fishing and running Kuyima, a local ecotourism company.

Raul's goal is not simply protecting a world-class coastal wetland. "I am very proud of what we did," he told me. "We helped preserve the right of local people to work their land, and we have made sure there is access to the public. There are no fences keeping people out. There are some people who think that the only option is to build mega-resorts. But I think that those of us who live in rural areas surrounded by natural beauty have an obligation to preserve these areas for everyone."

Ideally, López's vision of a coastline on which people can live sustainably with nature will be exported to other areas of the peninsula. Otherwise there is little hope for preserving much of Baja California's wild coastline.

Part II

The U.S.–Mexico Border

This isn't the real Mexico. You know that. All border towns bring out the worst in a country.

—Charlton Heston as Mike Vargas in *Touch of Evil*

7

Searching for Cartolandia

Working on environmental issues in the San Diego–Tijuana section of the U.S.–Mexico border involves facing the poverty and shocking conditions of the colonias that fill the canyons and cover the hillsides of Tijuana. My childhood forays into the slums of Tijuana with my parents were repeated when I returned decades later in an attempt to understand how to clean up the pollution that plagues border beaches.

When I was a kid in the early 1970s, Cartolandia (Cardboardland), a squatter slum of more than 25,000 people, filled with houses of cardboard and plywood, occupied the Tijuana River bed. My father, a novelist-turned-filmmaker, made one of his first documentaries while in the graduate film program at San Diego State University on the conditions at Cartolandia. My mom dragged my three-year-old little brother, Nicky, around the colonia while my dad made his documentary.

President Luis Echeverría, Mexico's successor to strongman Gustavo Díaz Ordaz, paved the way for the razing of Cartolandia in the 1970s during the development of the Tijuana River Zone and the construction of the Tijuana River concrete channel. After being evicted, the residents picked up their belongings and moved east in the river valley to a new Cartolandia. During the winter of 1980, more than one hundred of the residents of the new cardboard colonia died when the Mexican government opened the gates of Rodriguez Dam one night after severe rains. Over twenty-five bodies washed up in Imperial Beach and Coronado.[1]

Today, the Cartolandia-style slums of Tijuana are harder to find than they were back in the '70s. But they still exist, blotting out the fantasy of Tijuana's industrial progress and modernity. These shantytowns have counterparts in Nairobi, Rio de Janeiro, Manila, Lima, and Lagos.

Tijuana, historically one of Mexico's fastest-growing cities, cannot begin to provide adequate housing for the middle class, let alone its poorest residents. So the poor build shantytowns in the canyons that ring the city and in the flood-prone watershed of the Alamar River, which flows into the Tijuana River.

One of these neighborhoods is located at the southern edge of Colonia Chilpancingo in eastern Tijuana. It is located just below the maquiladora zone that is southeast of the Otay Mesa border crossing. In the middle of the river that cuts through the neighborhood, are the pipes and gullies that spew out toxic sewage and waste from maquiladoras. The sewage flows through the shanties made of cardboard, blue tarps, and plywood that house Tijuana's poorest people.

I toured the colonia on an overcast winter morning. Even after years spent among the rural and urban poor of Mexico, Peru, Morocco, and El Salvador, the poverty still shocked me. What did not surprise me was how thousands of residents have made normal lives out of unimaginable conditions to make their existence as bearable as possible.

A family carrying vinyl duffle bags carefully picked their way across the sewage gully by hopping along a shaky stone pathway. A makeshift plywood footbridge offered a dry route across the waste-filled river. Children played in yards filled with ornamental plants, chickens, and ducks. Packs of dogs wandered the streets. A large red-tailed hawk perched on an electrical post.

The colonia sits on an old landfill. Plastic, tires, mattresses, rocks, garbage, and paper poked through the dirt. Water trucks drove through the mud streets. Two cowboys on horseback rode across the river. One of the horses became nervous around a passing truck and reared, almost knocking me into the sewage gully. Electricity is hijacked from utility poles by dozens of colorful wires that are strung to each house. A new subdivision of townhomes advertising security and tranquility abuts the north side of the colonia. New gated communities are pushing informal settlements farther east to canyons that are even more danger-prone.

As I surveyed the houses, a young mother dragged a stroller through the mud across the river. She did not notice that the stroller tipped over and her newborn dangled upside down, held in place by a safety strap. I ran over and righted the stroller and the baby. The mother managed to quickly unhook her child from the stroller. She then tramped through the mud clutching her baby to her breast. I followed, carrying the stroller above the mud to the drier mud of a nearby road.

As I drove out of the colonia, I thought about how our job as environmental stewards and guardians of the public trust is not to help corporations make a profit at the expense of the poor but to advocate for and to organize those who have no power. Those who fail to speak up and address the human suffering and environmental degradation along the U.S.–Mexico border are as complicit as those who profit from it.

8
Lucha Libre
Wrestling for Life in Tijuana

Persuading people to preserve the natural environment requires commu-nicating with them in a culturally relevant way. To reach out to a new audience, I based Wildcoast conservation campaigns around the Mexican sport of lucha libre. I spent time with one of Tijuana's premier wrestling families to learn more about this rich pastime in Mexico.

A few miles southeast of the Otay Mesa border crossing in Tijuana's Colonia Guaycura sits a narrow two-story duplex that houses a family devoted to the sport of Mexican wrestling. Two *luchadores*, Super Kendo and his nineteen-year-old son, Kimura, reside there and plan their days around the art of lucha libre.

Lucha libre is an authentic part of Mexican popular culture in which figures such as El Hijo del Santo (The Son of the Saint) and Blue Demon battle in front of vast crowds in Mexico and the United States. The sport is also popular in Japan. The wrestlers are masked superheroes who never reveal their identity; this links them back to a tradition of Mexican heroes such as pioneering *luchador* El Santo (when I was a kid, I watched one of his many films, *Santo en atacan las brujas*, on television, and it gave me nightmares for months). Lucha libre is rooted in the ancient tradition of masked figures from Mexican indigenous culture.[2]

My brother Nicky and I were obsessed with the Argentine version of *lucha* when we lived in El Salvador in the mid 1970s. *Titanes en el ring* was a weekly television show with stars including La Momia, Don Quijote, Martín Karadagían, and the infamous La Momia Negra. We would use our allowances to buy stamps of the wresting stars to fill in our ragged *Titanes* collector's book. Just about every kid in El Salvador with access to a TV set loved that show.

I visited Kendo's home in Tijuana to encourage him to costar in a series of short marine conservation videos that Wildcoast was to produce featuring El Hijo del Santo, who had become our newest spokesperson. The idea was to use Kendo's longtime friend, El Hijo del Santo, the son of Mexico's demigodlike wrestler, El Santo, to star in a series of short

A poster for the Defiende el Mar (Defend the Sea) campaign featuring lucha libre star El Hijo del Santo.

environmental films, *Santo contra los enemigos del mar* (Santo versus the Enemies of the Sea), to be shown in Mexican cinemas and on YouTube. Kendo in his new alter ego Pirata Rapaz (Rapacious Pirate) would be the foil to El Hijo del Santo's attempt to stop overfishing and promote marine protected areas. In the series, Santo also fought the Zombie Sea Turtle Egg Eater, Sewage Man, and Chupacaguas (Sea Turtle Eater).

Kendo, who is originally from the Dominican Republic (he moved to Mexico when he was fourteen), had recently semiretired after thirty-seven years in the ring. He now sews costumes for Tijuana's lucha libre community and trains a new generation of luchadores. The wrestler was unsure whether his old friend Santo would want to work with him again—they had had a falling-out over an undisclosed issue. So I went to meet with Kendo at his eastern Tijuana house to reassure him that Santo was delighted about their pending reunion.

After I arrived, Kendo and Kimura paraded around in full costume in the driveway outside the house to show me their moves. Kimura demonstrated his kung fu–inspired kicks in the driveway. Kendo grappled with his son. The elder wrestler put his arm around Kimura and said, "He began fighting two years ago. I am proud that he joined the tradition of lucha libre."

Kimura's mother, Eva, worries about her oldest son but dutifully watches all his bouts. In a hushed voice she told me, "It is hard to watch him fight, especially when he gets hurt."

A few nights later, I drove to the Auditorio Municipal in eastern Tijuana to watch Kimura in a lucha libre evening that featured wrestling stars Místico and La Parka. The auditorium was packed with families. An electric atmosphere in the air fueled fights between the *rudos* (bad guys) and the *técnicos* (good guys). A trio of luchadores including the three-hundred-pound Pancho Cachondo pounced on Kimura, completely squashing him.

Despite being pummeled that evening, Kimura brushed himself off and held his head high after his bout. I thought back to what he had told me at his house: "The fans tell me that I have charisma. And I feel like I do have charisma."

Unlike the ugly ring of Mexican politics and the heartbreaking world of crime-infested Tijuana, in the sport of lucha libre, the *pueblo mexicano* is number one.

9

Viva Luis!

Punk Rock and Politics on the Border

When punk rock hit Southern California in the mid to late '70s, it spread south across the U.S.–Mexico border to Tijuana. There, a vibrant scene reflected the anarchic reality of the U.S.–Mexico border and Latin America rather than punk's gritty origins in New York and London. When the politically charged music hit Tijuana, the entire city was a real punk rock universe. My adventures in the punk scene there later helped prepare me to navigate the treacherous world of border politics in my quest to clean up the Tijuana River.

Back in the early '80s, my friends and I spent many evenings roaming the streets of downtown Tijuana. We often ended up in the tiny apartment of Luis Güereña, the king of Tijuana's emerging punk rock scene. His eclectic scene, that he spent so much time nurturing, morphed into the groundbreaking music of Mexican ska-punk pioneers, the band Tijuana No!. Luis's band was the forerunner of a whole alternative music and art scene that emerged from Tijuana, which included the Bulbo media collective and the genre-busting Nortec Colectivo.

Luis was an intense, wiry law student and punk activist who wore a ratty black leather jacket and shepherded Tijuana's punk and alternative music scene from its infancy. Luis brought bands such as X, Dead Kennedys (a concert that my kid brother Nick, now a music critic at Rhapsody, attended when he was fourteen), and others across the border to play in Tijuana. Luis lived and breathed to fight the establishment and understood the corruption at the heart of the Mexican political system. He would never have dreamed of blaming poverty in Tijuana on globalization without first pointing a finger at the endemic corruption of Mexico's one-party state turned fragile democracy.

For Luis, punk rock was a vehicle to express his outrage at the upside-down world of the U.S.–Mexico border. The American middle class punks who visited Luis in Tijuana did not always understand his worldview. But Luis treated everyone the same—extending his hand in friendship without hiding his contempt for gringo poseurs.

Luis's natural punk persona was a strong antidote to the fake outrage of Southern California upper-middle-class punks. But beyond what anyone wore, what mattered to all of us was the energy, excitement, anger, and brilliance of the music that propelled us to rebel against the rising homogeneity and stale 1970s—think The Eagles and Grand Funk Railroad—and the emerging conservatism of the Reagan era in the early 1980s. The music of The Clash, 999, Buzzcocks, Dead Kennedys, Stiff Little Fingers, TSOL, Black Flag, Circle Jerks, Bad Religion, Minuteman, and the Gang of Four, among others, fueled our outrage at a society we felt was moving backward.[3]

That immersion into punk did more for my sense of how to deal with environmental issues along the U.S.–Mexico border than anything else did. The do-it-yourself attitude of punk with its guerrilla politics and antiestablishment ethos was exactly what I needed when confronting multinational corporations or powerful government agencies. When other environmentalists stood back to see what developed, I propelled myself forward—just like a leap off the stage into the mosh pit (although my stage leap at my only performance as a punk singer at a high school talent show resulted in a broken arm and a suspension).

I last saw Luis in the early '90s at a Buzzcocks show at Iguana's, a Tijuana club. He had shoulder-length red and purple hair, wore his trademark leather jacket, and was handing out flyers for an upcoming concert. He still lived the punk rock dream. It was good to see him and learn later that he had done well with the seminal Mexican ska-punk band, Tijuana No! that launched the career of Julieta Venegas, a Mexican pop star.

Luis died in 2004, but I think about him a lot—giving him political stickers from Spain at his mom's house near Tijuana's notorious Zona Rosa, attending parties with freaked-out American poseur punks at his apartment, and talking to the rich girl from Pasadena he shacked up with (a Tijuana version of a Valley Girl).

One night in the early '80s, I left the *callejón* (alley) that fronted Luis's apartment off of Avenida Revolución in downtown Tijuana. Luis stood there in his leather jacket pointing to the chaos of Tijuana. In his heavily accented English, he shouted, "You want anarchy. This is anarchy." Rest in peace, Luis.

10

Waiting for the Border Watchers

In 2006, the U.S. Department of Homeland Security began building the first phase of its new "triple" border barrier near the Pacific Ocean in San Diego County. Environmental laws were waived due to homeland security considerations.

Smuggler's Gulch is a narrow garbage-filled canyon just east of the Pacific Ocean that is divided by a ragged and rusty metal U.S.–Mexico border fence. The small canyon is ground zero for the Bush administration's latest attempt to turn Tijuana into East Berlin. A massive earthen border barrier is under construction there, guarded by anti-immigrant Minutemen or others, who dutifully carry out alien patrols like Mulder and Scully of the *X-Files*.

If the border watchers had arrived in August, they could have caught Dave Smith, who was shot across the border fence at Border Field State Park by a cannon manned by Javier Tellez as part of the inSite border art festival. While hipsters applauded Smith for his daring, Border Patrol agents later issued a citation to Dan Watman for protesting fence construction at Border Field with a hand-scrawled cardboard sign that said, "Let's be friends."

I suspect that Michael Chertoff, the former Homeland Security secretary for the Bush administration, approved spending between $30 million and $60 million to build a giant triple Berlin-style wall in Smuggler's Gulch because he anticipated that Mexican performance artists would continue to bombard the United States with human cannonballs. I wish that Javier had instead shot Dave across the levees in New Orleans to waken Chertoff from his slumber.

Former congressman Duncan Hunter (R–El Cajon) believed that this transplanted Berlin Wall was necessary to fence off Tijuana, because Al-Qaeda operatives might sneak through the gulch on their way to bomb nuclear submarines in nearby San Diego Bay. From where I stood in the gulch one afternoon, I did not see any terrorists or *mojados*. The only sign of life was the mangy grayish black mutt that stared at the fetid water that flowed under the border fence. In their quest for jobs, migrants cross the border in the scorching heat of the Sonoran Desert over a hundred miles to the east. Thousands have died.

Hopefully the Minutemen will hunt the terrorists down with the ferocity they use to capture illegal alien gardeners and auto mechanics. More than likely, terrorists hitch rides with members of Mexican drug cartels who drive across the border in their tinted-window SUVs, despite having their photos in the dozens of wanted posters that are plastered all over the San Ysidro border crossing.

As a child, I spent summer afternoons with my parents in the Tijuana Sloughs, a salt marsh north of the narco-deco mansions in Mexico that abut the border fence between Smuggler's Gulch and the Pacific. We shared Pismo clam cocktails with Tijuana residents who walked north up the beach from Playas de Tijuana. One night while camped in the Sloughs with my family, I awoke to my father explaining in his broken Spanish to a scared and skinny Mexican boy that it was several days' journey to San Francisco from San Diego.

When border crossers jumped our backyard fence a few miles from Smuggler's Gulch in the middle of the night while escaping the Border Patrol, which they did a lot, my father patiently unlocked our backyard gate and gracefully sent the migrants on their way. In his mind, my father was still the scared and fearful child who arrived in Miami from France with my Grandma Lotti and Uncle Roland on a tourist visa to escape the Nazis. Some of my great-aunts and great-uncles and their children were branded as illegals by the Nazis and sent to death camps.

After Chertoff's Wall is completed and the border watchers have returned to their homes, I will continue to work with my neighbors in San Diego and Tijuana to clean up the sewage that fouls our beaches and the garbage that litters the hillsides and colonias on both sides of the border fence. For those of us living the everyday drama of two worlds that collide, neither walls nor Minutemen will stop us from improving our binational community that is threatened by the ignorance and indifference of public officials far away in Washington, D.C., and Mexico City.

Construction of the U.S.–Mexico border barrier is ongoing.

11

Terminal with Extreme Prejudice

Fighting Chevron-Texaco's Invasion of the
Coronado Islands

In 2002, corporations such as Marathon Oil, El Paso Corporation, Chevron Texaco, Sempra Energy, and Shell began a race to see which company would be the first to build a liquefied natural gas (LNG) terminal in northern Baja California. The most problematic of these projects was the plan by Chevron-Texaco to build its plant adjacent to the Coronado Islands (also called Islas Coronados in Mexico), a wildlife haven offshore from Playas de Tijuana just south of the U.S.–Mexico border. More than any of the other proposed projects, the Chevron-Texaco plan would have significantly threatened endangered wildlife.

From the bluff overlooking Playas de Tijuana and the rusting iron fence that juts out into the Pacific separating Mexico from the United States, the Coronado Islands appeared as a mirage. Only a short nine miles offshore from the southwestern corner of California, the three sister islands in Mexico that constitute the Coronados are where elephant seals, harbor seals, and thousands of nesting seabirds make their home. Sadly, because Chevron-Texaco is seeking permission from Mexico's Environment Ministry to build a $700 million LNG terminal six hundred yards offshore from the islands, the wildlife of the Coronado Islands might not have much time left.

As I peered out over the ocean from the dirt bluff at the edge of the grassy picnic area of the now-abandoned Border Field State Park, I covered my left eye and turned my head to the right. I could see only the islands and the quiet empty space of the Tijuana Estuary National Wildlife Refuge and the whitewater of the Sloughs, my favorite surf break, where bottlenose dolphins are more common than surfers.

The world's largest colony of the nocturnal and threatened Xantus's murrelet (a species of auk) can be found in the Coronado Islands. They are within an easy flight of the world's biggest storm drain, the Tijuana

River—a concrete channel turned natural river mouth that routinely spews up to 300 million gallons a day of sewage-polluted water after it rains. Nothing could be worse for a wild animal than to be the neighbor of an oozing Third World river—except, of course, to have an LNG terminal built next door. In the case of a catastrophic accident, every living thing in and around the Coronado Islands would be incinerated in an explosion that experts liken to a small nuclear blast.

For the families wandering the low-tide beach, couples hiding in the afternoon shade of the fence, and a few waders in their rolled-up jeans, the beach and the Coronado Islands are a welcome escape from the leaking lead smelters, belching *colectivo* taxis, narco-discos, sterile maquiladoras, endless graffiti-lined boulevards, and the hum of the San Ysidro border crossing that propels a never-ending stream of vehicles onto Interstate 5 and the promised land of California.

From my hillside perch, I liked gazing at the islands and the Tijuana Estuary. They reminded me that despite the ugly scab of a border fence that cuts off the hillside shantytowns of Tijuana from the garbage-and-feces-filled Tijuana River, the dues I paid to protect this little corner of our coast were well worth it.

During the summer of my sixteenth year, in 1980, I sat with my friends Jack Burns and Tim Hannan in front of skip loaders along with a hard-core group of Sloughs surfers and Imperial Beach lifeguards in an attempt to stop the Tijuana Estuary from being turned into a yacht marina. While corrupt Imperial Beach police officers stood by, two shaggy thugs assaulted me. Former Imperial Beach mayor Brian Bilbray dumped a skip loader of water and rocks on us. Luckily, a California Fish and Game warden intervened and threatened to arrest Bilbray. The Tijuana Estuary is now a federally protected wildlife refuge.

I flashed back to the skip loader incident when I became angry after a Chevron-Texaco representative informed me that the company's proposed LNG facility would not harm the Coronado Islands at all. To a disbelieving gathering of Mexican and American conservationists at a lunchtime meeting at the Tijuana Estuary Visitor's Center in Imperial Beach, the oil company rep insisted that constructing an LNG terminal visited by giant tanker ships at the Coronado Islands would not disturb a marine area he referred to as "biologically sterile."

The Chevron-Texaco LNG terminal is one of five such projects planned for the coast and ocean of the Californias. If the decision is left to oil companies, LNG platforms and their miles of pipelines will obstruct blue and gray whale migration routes and snake through beaches up and down the Californias. These planned LNG facilities received less scrutiny from government agencies than would the construction of beachfront condos in Newport or Rosarito Beach. The Coronado Islands project is the only LNG terminal planned for an area that a coalition of conservationists and wildlife biologists from Mexico and the United States would like to see declared a Mexican federal protected area.

Mexico's Environment Ministry approved a required environmental permit for the Chevron-Texaco project in September 2004. I hoped that a legal challenge filed by a coalition of environmental groups from Baja California (with funding from Wildcoast) would hold back the $700 million project until we had the funding to file additional legal challenges (two more permits needed to be approved by the Mexican government for Chevron-Texaco to begin construction).

To slow down the rush to build coastal and offshore terminals, a coalition of twenty-five environmental organizations from the United States and Mexico wrote to California EPA director Terry Tamminen. The California LNG Stakeholders Group asked Tamminen to halt construction of LNG terminals until the economic, safety, and environmental considerations could be developed that protect the people and coastal and marine resources of California.

To document the impact of the Chevron-Texaco project, I boarded the *Mustang*, a San Diego sport-fishing charter boat, for a trip to the Coronado Islands. I was part of a collection of guides who were to explain to reporters, political representatives, and environmentalists from both sides of the border the impact that the Chevron-Texaco project would have on the wildlife of the Coronado Islands.

The trip was the idea of Greenpeace, partners in our battle to preserve the Coronado Islands. I jumped at the invitation to spend the day on the *Mustang* to explain to the press and elected officials why building a giant natural gas terminal next to a refuge for wildlife was not a good idea.

The boat sailed out from San Diego Bay on a muggy morning. At the helm was fishing boat captain Myron Ackerman. He was the only fisherman in San Diego to openly denounce Chevron-Texaco for planning an industrial project in the middle of one of the most important sport-fishing grounds in the region. The commercial sport-fishing industry in California is not afraid to angrily denounce conservationists for calling for marine protected areas off the California coast. However, when faced with confronting a giant such as Chevron-Texaco, fishermen remained silent.

Fog swirled around the *Mustang* as we headed out into open water, past the sandstone cliffs of Cabrillo Point and the entrance to San Diego Bay. The Coronado Islands were a forty-five-minute ride away.

On board, Bill Powers (a clean-energy guru from San Diego) and the Greenpeace team gave an overview of the Coronado Islands issue to about twenty-five people. After the talk, I walked up to the bow as the *Mustang* emerged from the cloud banks and the islands came into view.

The sight was made more wonderful by the presence of Greenpeace's *Arctic Sunrise*, anchored west of the southern island. As we came around close to the Greenpeace ship so that it was between the *Mustang* and the location of the southern island's future LNG terminal, I shouted to Bill excitedly, "Greenpeace is back!" After years in the wilderness of acting like every other big international environmental organization, the Greenpeace that a legion of ocean activists had grown up with—Zodiacs flying while dodging whaler harpoons—was back in action. Bill nodded his head in agreement.

While we slowly came to a halt, photographers snapped photos of the *Arctic Sunrise*, and I noticed the discomfort and squeamishness of the young assistant to San Diego congressman Randy "Duke" Cunningham, one of the most anti-environmental members of Congress. With his trucker cap on sideways and black surf company T-shirt, the rep was a typical twenty-something surfer meets frat-boy turned establishment. A day out on the water and the islands probably sounded like a good idea when he was back in the office. But from the stern of the *Mustang*, surrounded by Greenpeace staff, he must have felt like a hostage at a Michael Moore film premiere.

To my surprise, an inflatable boat appeared off the stern of the *Arctic Sunrise* filled with Greenpeace staffers and Mexican journalists, including a cameraman, from Mexico's Televisa network. The inflatable, which belonged to Greenpeace, moved into a cove on the northwestern shore of the island, and the *Mustang* followed behind.

Arturo Moreno, a young Greenpeace activist, stood up in the skiff and declared the Coronado Islands a national protected area. He then came alongside the *Mustang* for an impromptu press conference. Moreno said loudly, over the noise of the *Mustang*'s engine, that the Coronado Islands should not be developed. "Rather, they should be preserved as a natural area for the Mexican people."

Witnessing that old-school excitement for this new era of fighting corporate giants made me smile. At least for the day, the *Arctic Sunrise* and Greenpeace revved up our movement.

On the U.S.–Mexico border, the only open space we have left is due to efforts to keep our coastline free from the concrete jungle that surrounds us. Where will we go when our ocean is filled with industrial terminals and oil tankers? The answer, of course, is that there is no place else to go.

That is why every time I look out over the Coronado Islands and the Tijuana Estuary I vow never to back down.

In March 2007, Chevron-Texaco announced that it was abandoning the Coronado Islands project.

12

Brown Water on the Border

In the fall of 2004, North Pacific storms slammed Southern California. Storm-related flooding resulted in the massive pollution of beaches along the U.S.–Mexico border. After spending my activist youth dealing with the issue of cross-border pollution, I once again became involved in the smelly politics of trying to halt renegade sewage flows. Unfortunately, rather than seeking a cost-effective and practical solution to the problem, some San Diego County federal elected officials proposed a "magic bullet" sewage treatment plant to be built by Bajagua, a company with no experience in wastewater management. The company's political supporters blocked lower-cost and more-effective publicly funded sewage treatment plants.

From my sunrise perch on the sand dunes overlooking the chocolate-colored surf just south of the U.S.–Mexico border, the Tijuana River valley appeared as a wilderness oasis. Behind me was the Tijuana Estuary National Wildlife Refuge. I faced the whitewater of the Sloughs surf break.

While under the spell of this early morning scene, I had difficulty imagining that the valley is home to the Tijuana River. The garbage- and sewage-filled river cuts across the border with the destructive power of a dirty bomb. After the slightest drizzle, the river becomes a manmade chemical and biological weapon that threatens the health and safety of thousands of south San Diego County and Tijuana children, including my own two surfer sons, Daniel and Israel.

Within hours of a storm hitting the border region, Tijuana, a city containing close to two million people, spews a foul-smelling Amazon River–colored sewage plume out of the Tijuana River mouth that spreads over the ocean for more than twenty square miles. The fact that after twenty-five years, the surfers, fishermen, and children of south San Diego County and Tijuana still endure the foul stench of the Tijuana River is a dramatic example of how many officials of the United States and Mexico have consistently made the wrong decisions about how to reduce the volume of the pollution that flows onto the beaches of Tijuana, Imperial

Mexican soldiers on the beach at Punta Banderas just south of Tijuana.

Beach, and Coronado. The exponential growth of Tijuana, especially at its western end, where hillside mansions abut canyons filled with thousands of families living in cardboard and plywood shacks, has finally overwhelmed the infrastructure built at U.S. taxpayer expense in the late 1990s to deal with the border city's urban and industrial wastewater.

The beach city of Coronado, located fourteen miles north of the Mexican border, was once safe from the flow of polluted water from Mexico. That is no longer the case. Now it is the recipient of the toxic ocean pollution that was once the sole domain of Imperial Beach and Playas de Tijuana. Since 2004, Coronado beaches have been more frequently closed due to increasing levels of pollution from Mexico, forcing U.S. Navy Seals to routinely halt ocean training exercises there.

The irony of this situation is that many of the residents of the multimillion-dollar, high-rise condominiums of Coronado include some of the most influential power brokers of Mexico. The yellow beach closure signs that appear more frequently along the shoreline of the Emerald City (as Coronado is called) are a reminder that border pollution, the distress signal of urban poverty in Mexico, can reach even the wealthiest enclaves in the United States.

To solve the border pollution crisis, some elected officials advocated spending up to $600 million in federal funds to subsidize the development of a private sewage treatment plant to be built in eastern Tijuana and run by Bajagua, a company with no experience in managing Mexican wastewater. However, the Bajagua plant (the brainchild of Tijuana developer Enrique Landa and his northern San Diego County partner Jim Simmons) would have had little or no impact in stopping the rivers of sewage that flow out of Tijuana's poorest neighborhoods and into the ocean.

The fact that Bajagua was considered a viable option to solve the border pollution crisis at all is due to the estimated $650,000 in campaign contributions that the company made to San Diego–area congressmen and President Bush, as well as the hiring of high-powered lobbyists, including James Jones, former U.S. ambassador to Mexico. These campaign contributions and lobbyists gave the company an excellent chance of receiving a sole-source, no-bid U.S. government contract. According to the Project on Government Oversight, an independent agency that investigated Bajagua, the deal would not have allowed the American public to "be assured the funds will be going to the most qualified bidder."[4]

Fixing the sewage system in a rapidly growing Third World city such as Tijuana, which is beset with impoverished squatter settlements without hookups to municipal sewage systems, will require a community-based and not contractor-based plan that is flexible, decentralized, and adaptive, and that involves capturing and treating sewage at its source.

Our elected officials should permit the people most affected by transboundary sewage flows, not campaign donors, to prescribe and implement a publicly managed sewage treatment plan that is a good deal for taxpayers and results in cleaning up border beaches. Until that happens, Navy Seals and children, surfers, and fishermen from both sides of the border will continue to suffer from the ever-increasing flows of Tijuana's untreated sewage.

13

Hasta la Bye Bye to Bajagua

On January 29, 2007, the *Wall Street Journal* excoriated the Bajagua company and its sewage treatment scheme in Tijuana in a front-page exposé. Investigative reporter Scott Paltrow wrote in his lengthy article,

> Without any competitive bidding, the United States gave Bajagua LLC, a start-up company with no experience in treating wastewater, sole authority to build and operate a treatment plant in Mexico. The tale of Bajagua's success in getting the contract involves, among other things, well-timed campaign contributions to local members of Congress and other political figures. And when that didn't prove enough, Bajagua obtained backing from Vice President Dick Cheney and the White House, which cleared away opposition by federal agencies, several former senior federal agency officials say.[5]

Even *San Diego Magazine*, a publication known more for its restaurant reviews and socialite gala coverage than investigative reporting, ran S. D. Liddick's article "A Sewer Runs Through It":

> Something is rotten in the state of California, and the smell goes all the way to the White House. For 10 years, a bitter and polarized South Bay debate has festered over a controversial San Marcos company, Bajagua Project LLC. Fighting the company is a consortium of environmentalists and engineers who say Bajagua's plans are an unnecessary distraction, carrying an undisclosed price tag (up to $780 million) that will line the pockets of a group of well-heeled investors but delay work on the real issue: the pollution of South Bay beaches and ocean water.[6]

The combination of the negative media coverage of Bajagua and a large-scale grassroots campaign against the project (carried out by Wildcoast) destroyed any public and political credibility the project once had. The grassroots guerrilla "Clean Water Now" campaign built a diverse and vocal constituency and coalition that demanded immediate public sector solutions to the cross-border sewage crisis.

"Bajagua=Scam" and "Clean Water Now" skater and punk rock–style campaign stickers, billboards, signs, and bed sheets were plastered around the border region and San Diego County. Lucha libre wrestling events in which the wrestler "Wildcoast" fought the bad guy "Bajagua" enraged Bajagua lobbyists. Southern San Diego County residents sent thousands of letters, e-mails, and postcards to key congressional allies such as U.S. senator Dianne Feinstein (D–California) and San Diego congresswoman Susan Davis (D–53rd District) opposing the Bajagua contract.

As a result of the "Clean Water Now" campaign, Senator Feinstein included $66 million in the federal budget for an alternative secondary sewage treatment plant to be built on the U.S. side of the border. She also requested that the U.S. Government Accountability Office (GAO) compare the cost of building a treatment plant in the United States (estimated at $100 million) with that of building the Bajagua project (estimated at between $600 and $780 million). A sewage treatment plant was originally planned to be built in the United States, but millions spent by Bajagua on lobbying and campaign contributions convinced most of the San Diego congressional delegation that spending hundreds of millions more to build a similar treatment plant in Mexico was a bargain.

On April 24, 2008, the GAO issued a report that found "that the Bajagua, LLC project includes more unresolved issues" than a proposal to build a similar treatment plant on the U.S. side of the border.[7] As a result of the GAO report, Senator Feinstein swung her weight on the Senate Appropriations Committee to fund an alternative secondary treatment plant to be built in the United States. The International Boundary and Water Commission terminated the Bajagua project on May 15, 2008.[8]

The Bajagua case could have been a classic issue of privatization and public policy gone awry. Instead, the cancellation of the project demonstrated that some of the strongest environmental safeguards we have are our constitutionally guaranteed rights of free assembly and speech and freedom of the press. Grassroots activists and dogged investigative reporters took advantage of our democratic institutions and won a victory for clean water and our coastline.

The construction of a new sewage treatment plant is nearing completion on the U.S. side of the border, west of the San Ysidro border crossing. Three additional sewage treatment plants have since been placed online in Tijuana at a fraction of the projected cost of the Bajagua project.

Part III

Southern California

Keep your ugly, fu**in', gold-bricking ass out of my beach community.

—Leon Russom as the Malibu police chief in *The Big Lebowski*

14

Watermen

Tales of the Tijuana Sloughs

Beginning in the 1940s, when north swells closed out the coast, surfers from all over Southern California made the journey to a remote and desolate beach within spitting distance of the Mexican border. Before the Malibu, San Onofre, and Windansea gangs began to surf Makaha and the North Shore, they experienced the thrill and fear of big waves at the Tijuana Sloughs, just north of the U.S.–Mexico border in Imperial Beach.

Surfers interested in riding big waves would get a phone call late at night: "Surf's up." The next day, they would show up at the county lifeguard station at the end of Palm Avenue in Imperial Beach. Dempsey Holder, a tall and wiry lifeguard raised in the plains of West Texas, and the acknowledged "Dean of the Sloughs," would greet them with a big smile. For Dempsey, the phone calls meant the difference between surfing alone and surfing in the company of the greatest watermen on the coast.

Boards were quickly loaded into Dempsey's Sloughmobile, a stripped down '27 Chevy prototype dune buggy that contained a rack for boards and a seat for Dempsey. Everyone else hung on for dear life as they made their way through the sand dunes and nervously eyed the whitewater that hid winter waves that never closed out. The bigger the swell, the farther out it broke. Surfers not uncommonly found themselves wondering what the hell they were doing a mile from shore, scanning the horizon for the next set, praying they wouldn't be caught inside, lose their boards, and have to swim in.

If you liked big waves and were a real waterman, you would paddle out with Dempsey. No one held it against you if you stayed on shore. Some guys surfed big waves, others didn't. It was that simple.

I first met Dempsey when I was a kid and got to know him better in 1981, when I became an Imperial Beach lifeguard at the age of seventeen. Retired, Dempsey lived in a huge wooden white house on the beach (appropriately called "The White House") a couple of doors down from the old Imperial Beach lifeguard station at the end of Palm Avenue. One summer Dempsey cleared out the laundry room and charged me a dollar a day to stay there. In 1984, I interviewed Dempsey for an oral history project while an undergraduate at UC–San Diego. By listening to his stories for hours, I uncovered Dempsey's remarkable history of athletic prowess and his unique depression-era way of looking at and respecting the ocean.

To gather material on the Sloughs, I spent a summer interviewing surfing pioneers and legends such as Peter Cole, Lorrin Harrison, Flippy Hoffman, Dorian Paskowitz, Ron Drummond, and others who had surfed with Dempsey. I was impressed by their admiration for Dempsey's surfing skills and ocean prowess. Dempsey, who was a generous and kind man, died in 1997 at the age of seventy-seven.

Dempsey mentored a generation of surfer environmentalists in Imperial Beach. They defeated plans in the 1980s to build a yacht marina in the Tijuana Estuary and a federally funded breakwater project just north of the U.S.–Mexico border. This oral history of the Sloughs partially influenced the decision by Kem Nunn to base *The Tijuana Straits* at the Sloughs and in Imperial Beach. That led to his involvement with David Milch and the production of HBO's *John from Cincinnati*, which was filmed in Imperial Beach and included a reference to Dempsey Holder. The historic contribution of the Sloughs to surfing history also strengthened our effort at Wildcoast to nominate the unique cobblestone reef at the Sloughs as a State of California marine protected area.

The Sloughs

Bill Hadji: When the winter storms came in, well, people know what it was like down there. The first thing they talked about was, "Let's go down to the Sloughs."

Mickey Muñoz: It's some of the biggest waves on the coast. The outside surf break is pretty awesome.

Peter Cole: The Sloughs had the biggest waves of any place in Southern California. It doesn't have the jack-up of a place like Todos Santos or the North Shore, but it's comparable to the outer reef breaks in Hawaii. It's really an impressive wave.

Richard Abrams: Way outside where eelgrass and kelp won't grow, it's just big boulders. It's all in one pattern and it focuses the wave. The whole thing is just bending around and hitting cobbles that are way the hell out there. When you get inside, there are smaller cobbles with some bigger cobble, and some eelgrass. That whole river valley contributed to that break. All those cobbles formed it.

Dempsey Holder: I had told the guys up north about the surf down here. They were asking about it. One day I stopped at Dana Point on my way back from L.A. with a load of balsa wood to make surfboards. It was the biggest surf they had here in six years. They wanted me to compare it, and I told them, "Well, the backside of the waves were bigger than that, bigger than the frontsides."

First Encounters

Back in the early 1930s, surfing was practiced at only a few beaches in Southern California. There were no wet suits. Dempsey Holder braved the frigid waters down by the U.S.–Mexico border to surf the Sloughs. He traveled the coast inviting his surfer friends to join him there.

Dempsey Holder: In the summer of '37 I went down to the Sloughs and camped with my family. Well, I saw big waves breaking out at outside shorebreak and went bodysurfing. I never did get out to the outside of it. A big set came and I was still inside of it. Well, I sort of made note of that. Boy, you know surf breaking out that far.

Lorrin "Whitey" Harrison: Back in the early '40s, I surfed the Sloughs when it was huge. It was all you could do to get out. Really big. We were way the hell out there. Canoe Drummond came down.

Ron "Canoe" Drummond: We pulled out and the surf was probably about twenty feet high or so. I looked out about a mile and there where some tremendously big waves were breaking. I asked if anybody wanted to go out there with me, but nobody did. So I went in my canoe and paddled out there.

Jim "Burrhead" Drever: One time about 1947, I was sleeping in my '39 convertible right on the beach at Windansea, and I heard these guys pounding on the car. I'd heard about the Sloughs and they were going, so I followed them. It was pretty damn big. This was before I went over to the Hawaiian Islands, and I'd never seen waves that big around here.

Peter Cole: I was out there surfing with Chuck Quinn and Dempsey Holder in the '50s. The surf was about fifteen foot, Hawaiian size. Chuck and Dempsey went out and got stuck in the shorebreak, but I managed to paddle out in the rip. I was out riding the smaller waves, when I heard someone yell, "Outside." I looked out and all I saw was whitewater everywhere. I lost my board and had to swim in.

Chuck Quinn: We were out there surfing on a big day and Pat Curren lost his board. Pat was frustrated and feeling lousy. He didn't have any money and it wasn't like today when they break a board and go buy another one. We all looked for Pat's board, but that board just disappeared.

The Phone Call

Lots of famous surfers, including Townsend "Towney" Cromwell, caught waves at the Sloughs with Dempsey. A Scripps Institution of Oceanography researcher who discovered what was called the Cromwell current in the equatorial region of the Pacific Ocean, Cromwell also had a U.S. government ocean research vessel named after him.

Dempsey Holder: One of the first guys that surfed down here was Towney Cromwell. He was studying oceanography at Scripps Institution of Oceanography.

John Blankenship: Dempsey called Towney in the early morning, and he could hear the roar of the surf in the background.

Dempsey Holder: Towney had gone over the depth charts and called me up and told me the bottom out there looks really good. I said, "Well, I told you about it." And he said, "You let me know when it comes up."

Jack "Woody" Eckstrom: Towney comes up and comes out and tells me, "Hey, Woody, you know that Sloughs is the biggest thing I've ever seen on the coast here. It's the biggest stuff I've ever seen. Dempsey is gonna give us a call when the surf comes up."

Dempsey Holder: About a week later it came up. I called Towney and he came down and got a lot of waves. The next day he came back and brought a kid from La Jolla named Woody Eckstrom.

Jack "Woody" Eckstrom: Dempsey called me and was real grave and said to Towney, "I think it's gonna be our golden opportunity." Towney looked at me and grinned from ear to ear.

The Ironman

Dorian "Doc" Paskowitz: There are two kinds of surfers. There's the Buzzy Trent type who surf big waves but aren't really into walking the nose. Then there's the Phil Edwards types who are blessed with amazing ability. Their surfing is like ballet. Dempsey was a big wave surfer. A big solid guy. Low-key. Not much for bragging.

Dempsey Holder: Back in West Texas where I was raised there were lots of cowboys, but that didn't mean too much. The thing that was a real compliment was to be a stockman. That's like a waterman—somebody that can handle themselves in the water. Emergency come along—you can take care of yourself.

Flippy Hoffman: Dempsey was the guru down there.

John Elwell: Around '47, '48, we met a guy named Storm Surf Taylor. He said, "Go down there and see Dempsey if you want to start surfing." Dempsey was known as the guy who takes off on big waves. He'd been down at the Sloughs since 1939.

John Blankenship: Dempsey was just unbelievable. There wasn't anybody else for sheer guts. He was the ultimate big wave rider. No fancy moves. He caught the biggest waves and went surfing. The closest guy to Dempsey was Gard Chapin, although Gard never tackled waves as big as Dempsey.

Bobby Goldsmith: Dempsey was an ironman. He was out there pushing through the biggest, goddamnest shit. He was fearless and brave and he had the guts. He took off on anything and could push through anything in any kind of surf.

Chuck Quinn: Dempsey rode the biggest waves back farther than anybody.

Buddy Hull: He'd take off even if he only had a twenty percent chance of making it. Dempsey would take off on anything, always deeper than he should have.

Jack "Woody" Eckstrom: I remember him saying, "If you make every wave you're not calling it close enough."

The Big Day

Today, modern surfers ride giant waves with high-tech wet suits and cutting-edge surfboards. Some are towed into huge waves by jet skis and ride specialized surfboards that are a hybrid of surfboard and wakeboard. Back in the 1940s, surfers had no wet suits and were completely on their own at the Sloughs if they lost their surfboards.

Kim Daun: In the winter of '43, I was in the Merchant Marine and just come back from a six-month trip. I hadn't been doing any swimming or anything, and I wasn't in the greatest of shape. Dempsey called me and said the surf was up at the Sloughs and wanted to surf with me.

Bob Goldsmith: It was so goddamned big that day. So wicked. It was one of those days where you could see whitewater forever.

Kim Daun: Dempsey and I went out and the shorebreak was murder. Dempsey had a heavy board, and my board weighed ninety pounds. We were really a long way off the beach and we managed to get onto a couple of rides. There was a lull, but then Dempsey and I saw it at the same time. The Coronado Islands disappeared behind the swell. So we immediately started paddling out like crazy. Dempsey was a hundred yards north of me and I was on the south side. The first wave broke and I was over to the shoulder of the first wave and it got Dempsey. From that point on I never saw him again.

Dempsey Holder: I was trying to make shore, but they were so damned big. I was going like hell trying to get back in there and here's something as big as a house looked like it was gonna break on me. I turned around and dove as hard as I could to get in the face of it, and not have it break on me. I don't know how long that went on.

Kim Daun: I got over that first wave and the second one broke about fifteen feet in front of me. That wave took my board like a matchstick. My god, when I saw fifteen solid feet of whitewater roaring down on me, all I could think was, "Get underneath it." I finally came up. I don't know how long that goddamn thing rolled around. When I came up, I was tired. The next wave busted in front of me again, and I went down and I thought I was deep enough and it still got me and rolled me and rolled me. The next goddamn wave broke right in front of me again, and this time I went down to the bottom and it was all eelgrass and rocks. I grabbed two big handfuls of eelgrass, and that thing just tore me loose from that.

Dempsey Holder: The horizons tilted on me a couple of times, and that scared me. The next time I didn't even look around. I just kept going. It broke on me and washed me far up enough so I could dig in. My eyes had dilated and everything was sort of puffy.

Kim Daun: Each time these waves came I would swim south as much as I could in the few seconds that I had. The next wave I got far on the shoulder and I swam south.

Dempsey Holder: Bobby Goldsmith shoved my board over to me and said, "Where's Kimball?" I said, "I don't know, we got separated. He took off left and I went straight in." He was supposed to be out of shape. I was supposed to be in good shape. I usually didn't get so tired, but when you don't have a wet suit on, your feet get a little numb, and the eyesight is a little fuzzy. I remember lying across the hood of a car, a Ford convertible, trying to get some body heat in. Bobby kept looking for Kimball Daun. Couldn't see him anywhere. Well, I said, "Goddamnit, maybe he drowned. Who do we let know? We're the lifeguards. Maybe we let each other know."

Kim Daun: I just kept swimming south. I was on the beach and they didn't see me. I came in south of the Tijuana River. I was freezing. I started walking on the beach, and they didn't see me until I got to the mouth of the river.

Bob Goldsmith: We waited there on the beach for Kimball. I hadn't been worried about Dempsey—old Ironman. I knew he'd make it. We were concerned for Kimball.

Kim Daun: I think I was as close to dying as I ever was in my life that day.

Bob Goldsmith: During those days it was every man for himself.

Simmons

The introverted, brilliant, and eccentric Bob Simmons, credited with applying hydrodynamic principles to surfboard design, started surfing the Sloughs with Dempsey in the late 1940s. Simmons hung out and shaped surfboards in Imperial Beach until his untimely death surfing La Jolla's Windansea beach on September 26, 1954.

> *Jim "Burrhead" Drever:* I used to say to Bob Simmons, "You're making a big mistake up here. You should go down to the Sloughs. They're bigger waves." He would never believe me. Finally he went down there and he met Dempsey and he hung out down there.
>
> *Chuck Quinn:* During Christmas vacation, 1949, I met Dempsey on the beach near the river mouth. He invited me to go surfing with him. A group of guys were coming down from Windansea and San Onofre. The next morning we met at the lifeguard station. As we're gathering, Dempsey said a guy had come down there the day before and had a light board tied to the roof of his car. Dempsey said, "I told him about the Sloughs and he drove on down."
>
> We got down there in Dempsey's Sloughmobile and saw a '37 Ford with the back windows painted, a board rack screwed to the top with some quarter-inch ropes tied to it. The board was gone and we figured

whoever it was, was already out there. It was big that day. Low tide, north swell, and of course, from shore we couldn't see it.

I'd never experienced anything as tough as that shorebreak. So Dempsey said to me, "Stick with me and I'll tell you when we'll go." I barely got through that last wave of set shorebreak.

It seemed like we were paddling out for half an hour, and there was still no sign of anybody. We got out and Dempsey says, "Geez, I'm looking for that buoy. I don't know where it is." Dempsey had put an old engine block to mark the lineup. Eventually we got out to where Dempsey says, "The buoy is gone. The surf must have carried it away. Maybe I didn't get it out far enough."

We're waiting out there, when all of a sudden we realized there was a huge set coming, and it was way outside from where we were. Dempsey tells us, "Paddle out, paddle out." We all started paddling furiously. I had never been in waves that big. These waves were just huge. We got over a couple of waves, but right away half the other guys lost their boards before we even rode any waves.

We were struggling, and I was holding on to my board. It's a wonder it didn't have hand marks on it. I was really scared and was in a situation that I had never even imagined. As we pushed through the next to last wave, here came this one lone rider on a huge wave. He was riding steeper and closer to the break than anything we ever imagined.

After the set we kind of regrouped and we're waiting for the next big set, when this guy comes out and paddles right through our group. Right into it. No one said anything. It was just quiet. We had heard about Simmons boards. There was a guy at Malibu that was making light boards out of balsa wood. So I said to him, "Say, is that a Simmons board?" He looked at me and he said, "My name is Simmons and this is my latest machine." And I remember when I turned my board I bumped his board. I was just a kid and I apologized. He just kept paddling.

John Blankenship: Simmons used to show up at Windansea and tell everyone, "If you guys had any guts you'd be out there with us at the Sloughs."

Shark Attack

Dempsey Holder: We had an El Niño kind of condition during the summer of 1950. The water was really warm, and there was a south swell—southern hemisphere swell. Made for some beautiful surfing.

Dr. Carl Hubbs, Scripps Institution of Oceanography, 1950: An unusual number of sharks have appeared in our waters as a result of prolonged southern winds.

Dempsey Holder: Bob Campbell, Jim Lathers, Dave Hafferly, and I went down to the Sloughs. Bob and Dave were bodysurfing. Jim had an air mat he wanted to try out there, and I took out my surfboard. I was the first one out. The other guys were real slow in coming out. They were at least fifty yards behind me.

All of a sudden I heard Bob Campbell holler something. Then Jim Lather hollered, "Shark." Bob hollered, "Shark." He had a real frightened tone in his voice. I was sitting there on my board thinking that he had come out here for the first time in deep water, and he saw a porpoise go by and just panicked. "Boy," I thought, "He's going to be embarrassed. He really hollered." Jim hollered at me again. It was a shark. I went over there but I didn't see the shark. There was blood in the water and Bob grabbed Jim's air mat.

San Diego Union, *Oct. 9, 1950:* A man-eating shark tore a chunk out of the thigh of a 31-year-old swimmer off Imperial Beach yesterday morning in what may be the first shark attack ever reported in local waters.

Dempsey Holder: I put the board right underneath him and took him in. Got bit. I'm sure he pulled his legs up. He had marks on his hands. He said it got him twice. Jim Lather saw it. He said it looked like two fins and then it rolled over. We didn't take long. Everybody was on shore. I took him on my board. He was bleeding from his legs. We took him to see Doc Hayes. He had a little office in the VFW. Bob looked kind of weak. He had that gray look. That shark must have taken a chunk of his leg the size of a small steak.

Passing the Torch

Low-tide morning. Offshore wind. January. The sun rose over the Tijuana Estuary. I sat on the rocks watching waves feather for hundreds of yards as Mike "Duck" Richardson took off, making his trademark bottom turn with a subtle hint of a soul arch. Racing around a section, he kicked out, grabbed his board, and headed back out. No one surfed the Sloughs better than Mike Richardson. Like Dempsey, fifty years earlier, most of the time the Duck surfed the Sloughs he was alone.

Mike "Duck" Richardson: When I was a kid, it was terrifying, but it was thrilling. It's still scary, but now it's like home. I can't wait for it. Sometimes I paddle out there when it's not breaking. Just to look around and sit.

Jeff "Spiderman" Knox: The Duck has a sixth sense about waves at the Sloughs. He follows the speed line. He'll always be in the best part of the wave. The bigger the Sloughs is, the better he does.

Mike "Duck" Richardson: I had just built myself a ten-foot pintail. It was a glassy winter afternoon. The surf was building and the wind dropped. I was surfing all by myself. Randy Coutts paddled out and told me that Dempsey was on the beach and had said it was the prettiest he'd ever seen the Sloughs. I guess Dempsey was up there watching me surf. And for Dempsey to say that. I thought it was good, but I didn't know.

The surf was magical. Real calm. And the sun was coming through the backs of the waves. Not glassy smooth. Light ripply smooth. Where you can see the texture of the wave, and you can hear your board chatter. There were ten wave sets. Waves were going to waste.

I try to get people to go out with me. But there are a lot of times when the surf comes up—everyone has to wash their car or cut the grass. I don't want to go out by myself but I'm not gonna miss it.

After breaking through the shorebreak, I wasn't sure if the figures bobbing up and down were pelicans or people. Beautiful green walls lined up all the way to the channel. As I arrived at the lineup, Duck paddled outside and caught the first wave of the set. I barely made it over the top. Paddling hard, I swung around, then paddled down the face of the second wave, a giant bowl and the biggest wave I had ever ridden. Wind was pushing up the face. Feeling my momentum gaining, I rushed toward the bottom, feeling the sensation of speed and weightlessness every surfer lives for. As I descended, I was outside looking in as the wave broke over me. Time stopped and then I emerged from the barrel, turned around the section towering above me, and raced down the line. Riding the wave until it died, I kicked my board in the air, yelling with delight. I was part of the Sloughs.

15
Indian Summer
A Surfer's Guide to the Fall

I t always irritates me when I hear recent transplants to Southern
California complain about the lack of "seasons" here—as if anyone
could fail to tell the difference between waves created by Baja California
hurricanes, southern ocean storms, and the thumping powerful north-
western Pacific swells that pound California beaches during the late fall
and winter.

Surfing in the fall means the difference between the opaque glassy
mornings of summer and the stiff and brisk offshore dawn patrols and
stunning sunrises (something hard to see during the overcast summer
mornings). The arrival of the Santa Anas is the California equivalent of
an Indian summer in New England. That is when the California coastline
becomes harsh and bright with hot offshore winds and the hillsides turn
crimson from wildfires.

When I was a child growing up in Los Angeles, my European immigrant parents reveled in the subtle California seasons that kept us on the
beach year-round. I spent fall weekdays with my mother on the beach
in Santa Monica. Weekends were spent at secluded beaches in Malibu,
where I loved watching my surrogate uncle, or *tonton*, Edmund Goutin,
a French immigrant and headwaiter in Beverly Hills, bodysurf the shorebreak. During hot afternoon winter weekends, my parents ventured to
Venice Beach, where the hippies loved my father's painted wooden Dutch
clogs and my mother and I swam across the canals.

The fall surf season that takes place in crisp, clear, hot afternoons with
clean west swells brings back memories of my childhood beach days.
When the first real northwestern swells arrive in early November, they
remind me of the excitement I felt when I started surfing. During that
epic 1977–78 winter, the surf pumped nonstop.

Sampling the strength of the first winter swells reminded me that
there is a big difference between the power of everyday waves in Southern
California and the surf delivered by North Pacific storms. On the morning of this season's first north swell, I watched my two sons surf overhead

closed-out waves on the north side of the Imperial Beach pier with the local high school surf P.E. class. Daniel (age nine), my youngest, never made it into the lineup and returned to shore before getting washed into the pier pylons. Israel (age eleven), my oldest, scratched into a few closeout set waves. It was a morning on which the boys understood my insistence on their daily workouts with the local swim team. Children who surf need to be very good swimmers.

Later that day, I paddled out for a brief lunchtime session at La Jolla Shores. The difference between the single twenty-something rippers in California and the rest of us married with kids trying to stay in the game is the minimal time we have for off-peak weekday sessions. I caught a few shoulders and fun drops.

Three days later on Sunday morning, the swell came up again and I dawn patrolled solid four- to six-foot offshore peaks in Imperial Beach with my sons. I caught a memorable barrel and experienced a late-takeoff pitch into oblivion that snapped my surfboard. One of the hard lessons I have learned (as a forty-something surfer learns while trying to stay in the game at a crunchy beachbreak with a crew of guys half my age who rip) is that I inevitably humiliate myself by blowing the drop on a hollow set wave when everyone is watching. I then paddle out to the lineup to the embarrassed silence of the crew, half of whom are pissed because I blew a good wave and half who feel sorry for me for turning into an aging kook.

When everybody else was watching the San Diego Chargers game later that afternoon, the boys and I bypassed the washed-out Point Loma and La Jolla reefs and were rewarded with a minimal crowd, beautiful blue skies, warm water, and some fun head-high waves at La Jolla Shores. Any true San Diego local knows that the best time to surf here is during Chargers games, especially during the playoffs, when beaches empty out. Once during a late-season playoff game we were rewarded with overhead waves at an almost empty Windansea in La Jolla on a sunny and glassy afternoon.

So turn off the football games and avoid the mall. Grab the kids and go for an Indian summer stroll along the beach. Real Californians know that summer is the worst time of the year; it is just a holding season until the ocean and the coastline really come alive in the fall. We are lucky that our coastal seasons allow us year-round access to the unpredictable Pacific Ocean, which truly defines Southern California.

16

Saving the Seals of La Jolla

Beginning in 1999, a small group of residents in La Jolla, a wealthy enclave of San Diego, became upset by the presence of a small group of once nearly extinct harbor seals on the postage stamp–size Casa Beach. These influential antiwildlife activists waged a political and legal battle to force the City of San Diego to rid the beach of seals. Unfortunately, the U.S. National Marine Fisheries Service, the federal agency charged with protecting the seals, ignored the plight of marine mammals under its jurisdiction. The conflict illustrates how difficult it is to convince California's political leadership that ocean wildlife are natural residents of the coast and ocean and not illegal immigrants.

Remarkably, in one of the most densely populated and most highly developed coastal districts in Southern California, a small population of harbor seals, once declared deadly vermin and decimated by the governments of the United States and Canada, now thrive. Approximately two hundred of these grayish-brown seals inhabit Casa Beach in the posh community of La Jolla.

In the spring, seal mothers give birth to their awkward but endearing pups at the tiny white-sand cove. Prior to the arrival of Europeans in North America, these animals could be found at rocky coves, estuaries, and sandy beaches throughout North America by the hundreds of thousands. Settlers in the New World slaughtered harbor seals for their oil and later for a five-dollar government bounty.

"Seal Rock," depicted in an 1887 map of La Jolla, is located where the existing seawall at Casa Beach now stands. By the time the seawall and beach were artificially created by the City of San Diego in 1931, commercial hunters had nearly wiped out the West Coast population of harbor seals.

In 1957, due to commercial hunting, the status of seals and whales along the coast of the Californias appeared so dire that Carl Hubbs, a Scripps Institution of Oceanography researcher, warned that if marine mammals were to recover, their habitat must be protected when they come inshore to breed. Thanks to the extensive lobbying of Hubbs, Mexico established reserves for whales, seals, and dolphins throughout the Baja California peninsula, while efforts to protect the animals in California lagged far behind.[1]

Today, the only locations in Southern California south of Santa Barbara where harbor seals give birth are at San Clemente Island and at Casa Beach. If the City of San Diego dredges Casa Beach, under a plan proposed by the Department of Parks and Recreation, San Clemente Island would be the only remaining harbor seal rookery in Southern California.

Under the proposed plan, the City of San Diego would spend up to $1 million to dredge sand from Casa Beach, which would theoretically result in greater tidal flushing and allow humans and seals to share a beach that would be much smaller than it is now. Paying for maintenance dredging over the next twenty years could cost hundreds of thousands of dollars. The fundamental problem with the Casa Beach plan is that if carried out, it would violate the Marine Mammal Protection Act signed into law by President Richard Nixon in 1972. Under Section 301 of the act, there is a moratorium on any actions that have the potential to disturb a marine mammal "in the wild by causing disruption of behavioral patterns, including, but not limited to, migration, breathing, nursing, breeding, feeding, or sheltering."

Dredging Casa Beach and opening it up to increased human use would have drastic implications for the population of harbor seals there. In many cases, if harbor seal mothers that have recently given birth are disturbed, they then abandon their pups. During a time in which the City of San Diego faces serious budget cuts, it is astounding that the Department of Parks and Recreation advocates spending scarce funds and staff time to placate a small, boisterous group of La Jollans who resent the harbor seals for inhabiting Casa Beach. Apparently, they cannot find any other beaches in La Jolla that are not inhabited by harbor seals.[2]

These activists are convinced that the harbor seals are to blame for allegedly increasing the population of white sharks in the waters off La Jolla and declining ocean water quality in the region. They are not aware that shark populations are declining worldwide. Marine scientists generally place the blame on humans and not seals for the alarming degradation of our coast and ocean.

Because public agencies spend millions of dollars annually to enhance wildlife habitat throughout Southern California, damaging the harbor seal rookery at Casa Beach would be a serious mistake. Children squeal with delight as they watch attentive but exhausted harbor seal mothers protect their newborn pups. Casa Beach is a wildlife sanctuary that should be permanently donated to the once nearly extinct population of seals that now call it home.

A new California state law signed by Governor Arnold Schwarzenegger in July 2009, to allow Casa Beach to be managed as a "marine mammal park for the enjoyment and educational benefit of children," will hopefully serve to stop the City of San Diego's dredging plans.[3]

17
The New Rockford Files Goes Blue

Watching *The Rockford Files* on Friday nights on NBC, starring James Garner as a Los Angeles detective, was a weekly event for my family during the halcyon days in San Diego from 1974 to 1980. Rockford's Paradise Cove trailer in Malibu was the perfect spot to get ambushed by muscle from the valley with bad hair and clunky cars. Jim's ex-con friend Angel Martin (Stuart Margolin) always embroiled the PI in his latest scam. Rocky (Noah Berry Jr.), Rockford's father, retiring from hauling big rigs across the USA, was the precursor to the NASCAR dad, with his cowboy hat and big pickup truck. And Beth (Gretchen Corbett) was the perfect attorney: she was great in the courtroom, always ready to bail out Rockford, and a hottie in a bikini. The plot always seemed to involve a mystery woman, a scammer extorting money, Rockford printing fake business cards in his '75 Pontiac Firebird to talk his way into the bad guy's lair, and a mobbed-up developer ripping off Rocky or one of Rocky's Teamster pals.

So here's the deal. I propose a modern remake of *The Rockford Files* set in San Diego with the PI as a surfing coastal crusader. Arnold Schwarzenegger would star as the new Rockford. His trailer would be located at Tourmaline Beach just north of the Pacific Beach pier. Instead of driving a Firebird, Rockford would style around in a biodiesel Volkswagen van. His hangout would be Moondoggies in Pacific Beach (as a replacement for the Paradise Beach Café), where he would drink beers with his surfer activist buddies. Maybe James Garner could make a few cameo appearances as Rocky.

Former congressman Duke Cunningham could be released from prison to play the hapless Sergeant Dennis Becker (originally played by Joe Santos), who was always confused, in trouble, and over his head. Rockford would get bailed out of jail with a little help and straight talk from Beth (played by Donna Frye, a surfing–environmental activist goddess turned San Diego City Council member and former mayoral candidate). The tough one is Angel, the Kramer of the '70s. That role would have to go to noted antienvironmentalist and northern San Diego County congressman Brian Bilbray. He is the reincarnation of Angel—making a mess of everything with his arcane and intricate dealings.

In the pilot episode, Rockford accompanies Rocky to a fancy hotel in downtown San Diego to help his father place a deposit on a Donald Trump condo in Baja California. Rockford becomes suspicious when he sees a picture of the proposed condo site and realizes that it is located next to the infamous Punta Banderas sewage river in northern Baja California. But when Rockford goes to the bathroom, Rocky writes a check for the condo.

Rockford travels to New York to get Rocky's money back. There he meets up with an old prison buddy, Carlos Sanchez (played by George Lopez). Rockford and Carlos confront sleazy Trump lawyers and PR flacks who threaten legal action if they persist in their quest for justice. Finally, they confront Donald Trump at a fancy environmental fundraiser where the developer confesses that his Baja project is a mess. Rockford calls a reporter friend, and Trump Baja is the subject of a front-page exposé in the *Wall Street Journal*. However, Rocky never gets his money back, because more than two hundred investors file a class-action lawsuit against Trump.

The second episode opens with Angel calling Rockford from a pay phone at the Del Mar Fairgrounds. The perpetually unemployed Angel lands what he thought would be an easy gig with the laborer's union. The job required him to attend a California Coastal Commission meeting and protest in favor of building a private toll road through San Onofre State Beach. Angel becomes worried when he realizes that many of Jim's Pacific Beach surfing and environmentalist buddies are protesting against the toll road.

Rockford's favorite nephew Rob (played by real-life surf star Rob Machado) is the leader of the anti–toll road group. Rob is the son of Rockford's sister Katie (with a flashback featuring Maria Shriver). A Japanese whaling ship killed Katie while she was trying to save a baby sperm whale. At the Del Mar Fairgrounds, Rob spots Angel carrying a pro–toll road picket sign. Rockford's nephew is angry that Angel would betray the memory of his mom, who dated Angel in high school. The activist loudly berates Angel in front of the other union protesters.

When Rockford arrives at the fairgrounds a little later, he stops two union thugs beating up on Angel and Rob. Angel had intervened to stop the thugs from pummeling Rob. Rockford's nephew urges him to investigate the toll road project to honor the memory of his sister. With the help of a contrite Angel, Rockford breaks into the Orange County headquarters of the toll road company. There the PI discovers secret plans to drill for oil in the state park as a way of raising money to stave off the company's impending bankruptcy. Rockford gives Rob copies of the plans. Rob hands over the oil drilling plans to *Los Angeles Times* investigative reporter Ken Weiss, an avid surfer, whose front-page exposé on the project earns him a Pulitzer Prize (and prevents his replacement by a sixteen-year-old blogger) and helps Rob stop the toll road project.

A few months later, Rob receives an environmental award from the surf industry at a groovy fundraiser in Laguna Beach. Rockford, Beth, Rob, and Angel celebrate their victory and Rob's award by surfing Lower Trestles, where the locals let Rockford catch a set wave even though he is not a pro surfer or a surf company rep.

Wouldn't *The New Rockford Files* be awesome? Each episode would end with Rockford leaving a confusing message on his answering machine, pumping up the volume of his retro 8-track player to blast Mike Post and Pete Carpenter's killer theme song with the wailing lead guitar all over the beach, and paddling out for a sunset surf at Pacific Beach Point on a Skip Frye fish.

With Rockford in town, San Diego would be so way back, baby. So way back.

18

The O.C. Meets *South Park* at the ASR

With the hordes of uninspiring elected officials who rule Southern California, it is hard to believe that our region shares the distinction of being ground zero for edgy action-sports youth culture. This is the alternative universe inhabited by the under-thirty crowd, who live for skateboarding, surfing, and snowboarding, in which politics is an echo of a universe that is as distant as the dinosaur age.

To tap the pulse of this new world in which youth culture is sold as a commodity of cool, the Action Sport Retail (ASR) Expo held every September and January at the San Diego Convention Center is the place to be. This is where the big guns of the surf and skate industry—companies such as Billabong, Reef, Rip Curl, O'Neill, Globe, Sector 9, Lost, Oakley, Globe, Vans, Volcom, DC, and Etnies—show off their products to retailers.

Orange County and northern San Diego County are home to many of the biggest names in the surf and skate industry that have built their brands as lifestyle and identity icons. These companies have captured the hearts and minds of our kids because they created a culture of cool that is more relevant than anything else the environmental movement has to offer.

The ASR is all about being a bro or a babe and entertaining the retail surf and skate shop owners. These owners then place orders and connect with the companies that keep them stocked with new lines and new ways for their customers to declare their originality to their friends who look just like them. The look now is all about the '70s and early '80s. Straight blond bleached hair, big afros, neon colors, dreadlocks, rainbows, and retro and green surfboards along with a new generation of sustainable surfboard and skateboard components are what is hip and happening.

On the floor of the convention center, company executives such as Billabong North America president and former pro surfer Paul Naude mingle with team riders, bikini models, DJs, and hip-hop stars including Paul Wall and Brooklyn's Supernatural. Hordes of up-and-coming surf and skate wannabe stars trying to score swag and possible sponsorships roam the aisles. Just about every company has its stars on display: Rob Machado, '70s surf legend Buttons, big-wave surfing icon Greg Long, skateboarder Tony Hawk, and longtime pro surfer and environmental activist Pat O'Connell.

There are dozens of other surf and skate luminaries whom my kids know and worship, though to me they look like every other teen and twenty-something with long, disheveled hair and wearing a trucker cap, surf sandals or sneakers, and a T-shirt bearing an undecipherable logo. My eldest son, Israel, cringed when I introduced myself to skate superstar Corey Duffel—who had a Richard Hell meets Keith Richards look of teased-out rock star hair, a black leather jacket, and a slim-fit black rock star T-shirt—and asked him, "So what do you do?"

Afterward, Israel said, "That was very uncool, Dad. Corey is, like, one of the world's most famous skateboarders."

While the surf world is still mostly white, upper middle class, and so very Malibu, with Orange County somewhere in the middle, skateboarding is diverse and egalitarian. Surfing in Southern California has always been about our ruling class gone a little haywire. Modern skateboarding has its roots in Santa Monica, L.A., Carlsbad, and anywhere else Jay Adams, Tony Alva, Gregg Weaver, and Tony Hawk set their wheels down.

On a Saturday afternoon at the Boost Mobile and éS Game of Skate contest, hundreds of Latino and African American kids watched the world's best street skaters on display. Skateboard companies realize that inner-city youth are a market they cannot ignore. But as my longtime friend Jim Flanagan, an Oakley sales manager, told me from the hyper-modern and very cool Oakley booth (in the way that only a DJ- and model-filled space can be), "This market is always about rebuilding your brand and reinventing yourself and constantly reaching out."

The Surfrider Foundation and Obama presidential campaign organizers took note of the grassroots and guerrilla marketing techniques of the action-sports industry so prevalent at the ASR. Surfrider's innovative and pop culture–themed Save Trestles campaign was an echo of the funny and irreverent Volcom marketing techniques. Obama campaign iconography riffed on action-sports and pop music imagery. It is no accident that Shepard Fairey's "Hope" poster and imagery along with will.i.am's "Yes We Can" music video became the symbols for Obama's campaign of hope and change. Fairey, who emerged from the underground skate world, applied the well-honed art of stickering do-it-yourself guerrilla

El Hijo del Santo giving a talk in Los Laureles in Tijuana.

politics to give the Obama campaign street cred and a lock on the youth vote. The will.i.am video was a perfect merging of pop music, celebrity culture, and politics.

I applied the same pop culture marketing techniques to Wildcoast environmental campaigns. A graphic artist with ties to the underground skate community came up with logos for a "Clean Water Now" campaign. We brought in lucha libre stars such as El Hijo del Santo to deliver environmental messages in Mexico and among Latinos in the United States. We toured with the Mexican rock band Maná and norteño stars Los Tigres Del Norte to promote our coastal and marine conservation initiatives. Using pop culture marketing techniques is crucial to broaden the audience for environmental issues.

So next year, let's get Governor Schwarzenegger and the entire state legislature to the ASR. They can hang with the crazy Volcom crew dressed as cavemen, talk Hurley Pro heat strategy with Dane Reynolds, check out their Facebook pages at the Roxy Girls booth, tweet about hanging out

A poster for the Clean Water Now campaign.

with the foxy Reef girls, and impress everyone that even though they pretend not to care about being cool—they desperately need to be.

Imagine if government was relevant to our lives, reached out to our kids, and allowed us to solve problems by surfing Black's or skating Washington Street with elected officials, instead of having to bang on smoke-filled backroom doors to speak with them. That would be very cool indeed.

19

From *Fast Times* to David Milch

A Brief Cultural History of San Diego

L ast week I spent a morning helping scout locations in the Tijuana River valley for HBO's new series about Imperial Beach: *John from Cincinnati*. The show is to be produced by David Milch, the creator of HBO's *Deadwood*. David is one of the most fascinating and loquacious personalities in Hollywood. He is co-producing and writing the series with Kem Nunn. Preproduction work has already started, and Milch's crew is building a set at a run-down motel on Highway 75 in Imperial Beach at the southern end of San Diego Bay.

I helped search for suitable locations with Brian Haynes, Milch's location manager. Brian is a longtime veteran of the Hollywood film industry and had great stories to tell (such as a promotional tour in Japan for *Star Wars* with Carrie Fisher). He worked on the cultish *Blade Runner* and the '80s teen epic *Fast Times at Ridgemont High*.

Fast Times is based on Cameron Crowe's book of the same name about his undercover stint at San Diego's Clairemont High, in which Crowe documented the fact that '70s teens were (gasp!) screwing, smoking pot, and drinking beer. Crowe also filmed his San Diego–inspired semiautobiographical *Almost Famous* in San Diego's Ocean Beach and at the San Diego Sports Arena. Talking about *Fast Times* with Brian and its connection to San Diego got me thinking about how the city has changed since I was a kid, back in the bygone and carefree days of the 1970s when San Diego was "America's Finest City."

Anyone who grew up in San Diego in the '70s is aware that Clairemont High, Patrick Henry High, Bonita High, and Grossmont High were the epicenters of Camaro-dude, Farrah Fawcett–hair, inland cultures where bongs, kegs, babes, and Van Halen ruled. Back in those days, going away to college meant living at home and commuting to Mesa College, San Diego State, or UC–San Diego in a Camaro, VW Bug, or Datsun B210.

That was when Pete Wilson was a normal and moderately good mayor (before he became an unpleasant governor) and before San Diego became overrun by chain stores and Starbucks. Downtown San Diego's Horton

Plaza was filled with prostitutes, winos, pimps, pushers, and vagrants. Visiting downtown San Diego at night meant a trip to the Skeleton Club, a punk rock haven, and a pre-show visit to hunt for rare promo-copy records at Arcade Music. The Brass Rail and the Chicken Pie Shop were the culinary and cultural epicenters of Hillcrest. And Kensington, now an upscale urban enclave, was a strange place filled with freaky teens who hung out at Kensington Park next to the Ken Cinema and were obsessed with Dungeons and Dragons and the British new-wave band XTC.

Unfortunately for our dear city, San Diego shed its Southern California roots and mojo. The city killed off the Skeleton Club, we switched from pot and beer to haze-inducing triple no-foam soy lattes, and voters ignored the nonstop John Tesh–inspired symphony of City Hall while sitting in traffic on Interstate 15. The recent 1970s retro surf revival, along with San Diego's centrality to skateboarding, has given San Diego some of its street cred back. That has done little to transform San Diego's stifling corporate political culture.

So to prepare for *John from Cincinnati* and to better understand the roots of Southern California's beach and skate culture, check out Stacy Peralta's brilliant documentary *Dogtown and Z Boys*. In the best film ever made about Southern California, Peralta dug deep to tell the story of the troubled group of teens he grew up with, who helped develop modern skateboarding. Then listen to a little bit of Black Flag, Suicidal Tendencies, Iggy Pop, and San Diego's own The Zeroes before watching the cult film *Repo Man*, in which punks, aliens, and a band of outlaw repo men come together to live in peace and harmony in the flood-control canals of Los Angeles. Hopefully, with *John from Cincinnati*, David Milch will return San Diego to its gritty roots.

20

HBO Invades Dogtown in Imperial Beach

My experience working on the production of HBO's John from Cincinnati, *filmed literally outside my office doorstep in Imperial Beach, illustrates how the real and surreal often blend together in coastal environmental campaigns. The fictional story of the Yosts, this HBO series featured a surfing father who fought for clean water (on YouTube) and a visiting angel or alien named John, who in one scene wandered through a real eco-wrestling match featuring "good" Mexican wrestlers fighting their archenemies, Sewage Man and Sea Turtle Eater, at Earth Fair in San Diego's Balboa Park.*

Back in the early spring of 2006, Kem Nunn called me to tell me that David Milch might film a new HBO series about Imperial Beach. At the time, Kem was a writer on HBO's *Deadwood*, a brilliant deconstruction of the West and the evolution of American civic culture and capitalism. Kem's description of *John from Cincinnati* sounded intriguing. The story involved a dysfunctional Imperial Beach surfer family, an alien, a weird motel, and lots of odd characters against the backdrop of the polluted U.S.–Mexico border. Kem thought there could be a role for Wildcoast in the production that would help to further our efforts to clean up the border. As a big fan of Milch, I jumped at the chance to find a way to include our environmental message in a television series that seemed like it would be a hit. Kem's *Tijuana Straits* had given our efforts to fight for clean water on the border literary legitimacy. I was hopeful that having Milch and Nunn explore similar terrain would provide Wildcoast greater visibility.

A month later, I found myself acting as a tour guide for Nunn, Milch, and a van full of the eventual producers, directors, and writers for *John from Cincinnati*. As we toured Imperial Beach and the Tijuana River valley, I talked about the history and geography of Imperial Beach and the U.S.–Mexico border. I also led them to a few places that became shooting locations for the show—Katy's Coffee Shop, the south end of Seacoast Drive, Goat Canyon, and Border Field State Park. I identified the El Camino Hotel as the location for the Snug Harbor Motel, the show's main set. The skid-row-style motel, with a menagerie of plastic life-sized forest animals around its empty swimming pool, had once been home to the infamous Vienna Lounge.

Soon after that first trip, Milch brought his cast and crew to Imperial Beach to film the series. Because the main set, the Snug Harbor Motel, was only a block from my house, I rode my bicycle over to say hello on most mornings that Milch was in town (he shot the interiors at Melody Ranch in Newhall, California, north of Los Angeles). I was astounded by the amount of crew and equipment that filled local streets.

John from Cincinnati, featured an eclectic cast including Bruce Greenwood, Ed O'Neill, Luke Perry, Austin Nichols, Luis Guzman, Brian Van Holt, Rebecca De Mornay, and even pro surfer Keala Kennelly. The show combined the California outlaw culture elements of Nunn's novels *Pomona Queen*, *The Tijuana Straits*, and *Tapping the Source* with Milch's theme of redemption that was present throughout *Deadwood*.

The Yost clan's patriarch, Mitch Yost (Greenwood), is a hideout from the world of commercial surf culture. His errant son, Butchie, a former professional surfer turned heroin addict (played perfectly by Van Holt) attempts to fleece the recently arrived John Monad (Nichols). Upon meeting John, Butchie is transformed from scammer to savior and becomes more human as he wanders the streets and surfs the waves of Imperial Beach with the stranger, who may or may not be from Cincinnati.

John from Cincinnati had plenty of *Deadwood*-style cursing that I found realistic. In a blue-collar beach town like Imperial Beach, you do not have to spend that much time with surfers to hear machine-gun expletives. But not everyone was happy with Milch's take on beach life or at least with the cuss words. One day on the open Seacoast Drive set, an elderly woman presented Milch with a petition to have him ban the use of foul language in the television series.

"Anyone who is from a working-class community knows that is how people speak," Milch told me over lunch with Nunn after the incident.

A few days later, I met up with a longtime local surfer while I was checking out the surf north of the Imperial Beach pier. "That HBO show has too many cuss words, goddamnit," he said. "It's all fuck, shit. Motherfucker, that show should be moved to National City or Chula Vista."

Overall, *John from Cincinnati* was a boon for Imperial Beach. The production team set a gold standard for how film crews should treat a community (although some residents, believing that it sullied the image of Imperial Beach, hated everything about the show). Milch and his crew hired many Imperial Beach residents as production staff and extras (including my two sons and dad and local Avon lady Rosa Adams) and opened up tabs at local businesses. Milch treated his team and local residents with an amazing amount of respect and interest. He is a warm, generous, funny, and talented person who established an atmosphere of risk and creativity that seems to be rare in Hollywood.

You never knew what to expect with Milch. Every moment was new and transcendent, which drove his crew nuts, because it meant continual last-minute script rewrites, continual shooting delays, and cost overruns. Milch's anything-goes demeanor helped me one day when I wandered over to the lunch tent on Seacoast Drive to pass out flyers inviting the cast and crew to a lucha libre event that Wildcoast was to hold for the Earth Day Festival in San Diego's Balboa Park.

Kendo, the Mexican lucha star, appears briefly in the opening title sequence of *John from Cincinnati*. The wrestler agreed to bring a team of wrestlers to Earth Fair in the name of preserving the coast and ocean. I gave a flyer to Milch. He looked it over and called over his cousin Mark Ostrick, who had been standing quietly in the corner of the tent. "Hey, we should film this," Milch said, handing Ostrick the flyer.

Ostrick organized a crew for the following day. They filmed a scene with actors Austin Nichols and Emily Rose during a lucha libre bout between Sewage Man and CostaSalvaje (Wildcoast in Spanish). There was no script. The scene was improvised and appeared in episode five.

The first two episodes of *John from Cincinnati* were quirky and funny. They revealed an idiosyncratic view of life on the edge along the U.S.–Mexico border, mired in the subaltern surfing subculture of Southern California. Brian Van Holt was excellent and true to life as Butchie. He nailed the mannerisms, speech, and look of a junkie-surfer-hoodlum. Ed O'Neill was amusing as the ex-Imperial Beach cop caught in confusion. Luke Perry was believable as a surf industry CEO. And Greenwood provided a quiet dignity in the role of Mitch Yost, the levitating former surf star turned Yost patriarch with a screaming spouse from hell, played by Rebecca De Mornay.

To further the show's blend of reality and the surreal, Milch had Ostrick, a documentary filmmaker, film the lives of Imperial Beach's eclectic residents and the show's characters for a series of revealing mini-documentaries and YouTube clips. The Ostrick video sketches featured an Imperial Beach punk band named The Resentments, two skaters who ride forgotten drainage ditches, pollution in the slums of Tijuana, and Sloughs surfer Mike Richardson talking about the art of crafting surfboards. Ostrick even filmed Greenwood as Yost in a fictional public service announcement for clean beaches that ran on YouTube and was later referenced in episode nine. The video sketches were never aired (but are now available at JFCexperience.com), however, and the YouTube clips never had a chance to reach the show's fan base.

Unfortunately, as many of the production team complained to me while filming, *John from Cincinnati* wasn't going anywhere that they or the audience could understand. After the third episode, I found the story almost impossible to follow. There just wasn't enough surfing, U.S.–Mexico border, and beach time. Milch also inexplicably turned away from the U.S.–Mexico border, a setting that would have infused the series with a much-needed dose of realism. Ironically, right after the demise of *John from Cincinnati*, the Showtime series *Weeds* moved its characters and setting to Ren Mar, a fictional border beach town modeled after Imperial Beach, and dealt with drug smuggling and illegal immigration.

John from Cincinnati was a gamble from the very beginning. Chris Albrecht, an HBO chief fired for assaulting his girlfriend, gave the green light to Milch. Unfortunately, the HBO executives who replaced Albrecht did not have the same faith in the show. About 1.6 million people per week watched *John from Cincinnati*; that viewership did not compare to the 10 million or so who viewed *The Sopranos*. After the first season ended, HBO cancelled *John from Cincinnati*.

After Milch and company left town, life returned to normal in Imperial Beach. There were no more afternoon surf sessions with Van Holt (who is a very good surfer) and big-wave surfer and water unit member Brock Little. Nor was there any more listening to the philosophy of Milch and the true crime stories of his larger-than-life business partner Bill Clark, a former New York City police detective turned Emmy-winning television producer and writer. Imperial Beach felt empty without the *John from Cincinnati* crew in town.

If you still want to capture some *John from Cincinnati* magic, head down the Imperial Beach Pier Plaza, step into the Cowabunga ice-cream shop, and order a scoop of *John from Cincinnati* ice cream. With a smooth mint flavor and sprinkled mocha chips, it is a great way to cool down on a hot summer afternoon. Then catch the sunset from the Imperial Beach pier while watching the lights of Playas de Tijuana and its beachfront bullring flicker south of the border.

21
Saving Trestles, Part I
Surfing with Schwarzenegger

San Onofre State Beach is home to some of the most iconic and best surf-
ing spots in Southern California. From the cobble reefs of Trestles, known
for their rideable and consistent waves, to San Onofre Surf Beach, one of
the original surfing areas of California, the state park is one of California's
most popular. A surfing rite of passage in Southern California involves
hiking the trail to Trestles that meanders past San Mateo Creek to reach
the beach or spending the day with friends and family surfing the mel-
low waves of San Onofre just south of Trestles. Lower Trestles, the site of
the only American stop on the Association of Surfing Professionals world
tour, is one of the global centers for modern surfing.

So when the Orange County–based Transportation Corridor Agencies
(TCA) proposed placing a toll road through San Onofre along the tranquil
San Mateo Creek, surfers joined forces with environmentalists to halt the
proposed construction project. I viewed the toll road not just as a threat to
a unique coastal natural area but as a dangerous assault on California's
heavily used and underfunded state park system.

When the Sierra Club's Owen Bailey contacted me about spending
the first-ever International Surfing Day on June 21 in Sacramento
to lobby against the proposed construction of a toll road that would bisect
San Onofre State Beach, my first thought was, "Dude, are you crazy?"

Although he is one of California's most dedicated coastal activists,
Owen is not a surfer. So he does not understand the first law of California
surfers—never, ever, ever, ever go inland during the summer.

There was no way that I was going to spend the first day of summer
and the first-ever International Surfing Day in Sacramento. Anything
beyond the geographical range of June Gloom was too far for me.

Realistically, however, the power center of California surfing is not
divided between Steamer's Lane in Santa Cruz and Trestles; the real
power center for making decisions about the future of surfing and our
way of life is in Sacramento. When it comes to deciding what beach will

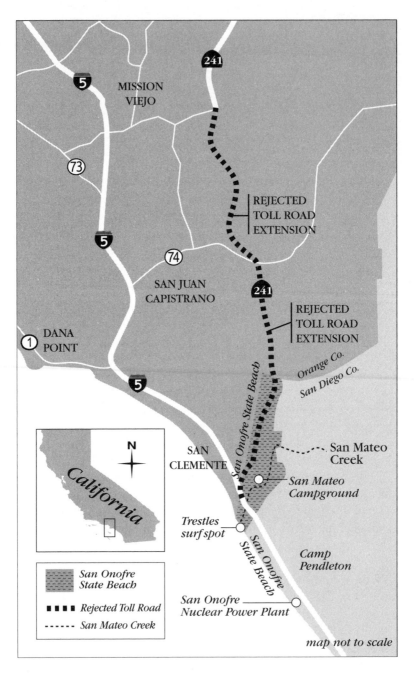

The proposed toll road extension in San Onofre State Beach

be developed, who will receive a pollution permit, and what tax monies will be authorized to conserve the coast, the suits and ties of Sacramento control us lock, stock, and barrel. Every developer, polluter, and power broker with an interest in our coast retains minions who move at breakneck speed around Sacramento. They influence legislators, agency bureaucrats, and the governor to make sure their interests come first and our desire to surf clean waves comes last.

If you want to save Trestles, Rincon, or Malibu, then get used to the idea that the power brokers will not come to you. You have to go to them. Better yet, get about a thousand of your best friends to sign a surfboard asking the governor to save your imperiled surf break, put on your best Hawaiian shirt, and hop on a flight to Sacramento. Then tell your story to every California state legislator you can find in the dingy offices of the capitol building about why saving surf spots is the most important thing they will ever do.

That is exactly how thirty of California's most passionate coastal activists spent the first International Surfing Day. We traveled there by plane, train, and automobile in the effort to save Trestles. After a midmorning briefing by the Sierra Club's Elizabeth Lambe, our group (which included *Surfer's Journal* publisher Steve Pezman and women's pro surfing pioneer Jericho Poppler, along with the Surfrider Foundation's Ed Mazarrella) made its way to the state capitol. There we wandered the hallways to meet every influential legislator we could find representing the California coast to ask them to sign a letter to Governor Schwarzenegger requesting that the toll road be stopped.

Trestles local Brian Alper, who had just returned from a surf trip to Costa Rica, passionately informed Val Dolcini (the director of policy for Lieutenant Governor Cruz Bustamante) why having the surfing pro tour visit Trestles was good for the economy. Stinson Beach surfer Scott Tye defended surfing and our coast to the staff of Joe Nation, a legislator from Marin County. In the end, thirty-eight legislators signed on to the "Save Trestles" letter.

The highlight of the trip was a visit to the office of Governor Arnold Schwarzenegger. We arrived with the signed letter and a San Clemente Surf Company longboard. The surfboard was signed by close to a thousand San Onofre and Trestles surfers asking the governor to save their beloved surf break from destruction by stopping the toll road.

We never expected to actually meet the governor, and the longboard almost never made it through security. In the end, though, the karma

Surfrider Foundation's Save Trestles campaign art riffing the Sex Pistols album *Never Mind the Bollocks.*

of our team spreading surfer cheer throughout the capitol must have worked. While we were waiting, Secretary of State Bruce McPherson, a former legislator from Santa Cruz, stopped by and told us of his experience surfing with Santa Cruz big-wave pioneer Richard Schmidt. Then, thanks to Schwarzenegger's cabinet secretary, Terry Taminnen, and his deputy, Drew Bohan—both good friends of surfers—we actually made it in to see the governor. And when Schwarzenegger came out into the meeting room, he shook our hands and talked about how Hawaiian surfer Gerry Lopez, who had costarred with Schwarzenegger in *Conan the Barbarian*, taught him to surf in Maui. "The waves were huge, and I spent four hours mostly swimming," he said.

We briefly touched on our talking points about why San Onofre needed to be preserved. I thanked the governor for passing the Ocean Protection Act. We invited Schwarzenegger to visit and surf Trestles. Then, after saying goodbye, about half our group retreated to the historic Crest Theatre for an evening of free beer and a showing of *Endless Summer II*. The rest of us returned home.

Even if we were miles from the beach, it was not a bad way to spend the first-ever International Surfing Day. Whether you spent June 21 surfing clean waves, picking up trash at your local beach, or talking to a government official about the need to conserve our coast, the fight to save Trestles and every other threatened surf break on our planet is far from over. But on the day when we showed the world that surfing matters, we proved that no one—and I mean no one—can defend our coast and ocean with as much passion as a surfer can.

22

Saving Trestles, Part II

Five Lessons from Big Wednesday

I n the annals of surfing history, there has never been another day quite like Wednesday, February 6, 2008, known as "Big Wednesday." That is when more than three thousand surfers, celebrities, politicians, bureaucrats, biologists, bird lovers, Native Americans, surf-moms, grommets, pro surfers, and surf company CEOs came together at Wyland Hall at the Del Mar Fairgrounds to stop what Mark Massara, the Sierra Club's Coastal Program director, called "the devil child of all coastal development projects."

Massara was referring to the plan by the Transportation Corridor Agencies to build a toll road that he said "would have destroyed San Onofre State Park, Trestles, Native American sacred sites, a public campground, a wildlife conservation refuge, an entire watershed, creek, wetlands and a dozen endangered species." The toll road project would have had a significant impact on the largely undeveloped San Mateo Creek watershed. The pristine state of the watershed is largely responsible for the first-class wave quality at Trestles and the wild feel of the spot, despite its proximity to Interstate 5 and hyperdeveloped Orange County on its northern flank. The road project would also have significantly impacted habitat for eleven endangered or threatened species, including the nearly extinct southern steelhead trout.

The decisive rejection on February 6 by the California Coastal Commission (8–2) of the proposed 241 Toll Road was one of the most significant events in the history of the California environmental movement. The people who assembled to defend San Onofre Trestles made up the largest crowd in the history of coastal commission hearings.

During this event, the Woodstock of the surf movement, you could feel what Stefanie Sekich (Surfrider's Save Trestles campaign coordinator) told me was "the energy in the air—a booming resonance of civic duty." Sekich said, "Seeing thousands of people come together in an orderly, positive fashion made me feel hopeful for the future."

Ben McCue of Wildcoast is interviewed by a reporter at the February 6, 2008, meeting of the California Coastal Commission at the Del Mar Fairgrounds regarding the proposed TCA toll road plan.

At 11:20 p.m., when the coastal commissioners voted to stop the toll road, it was, according to the Surfrider Foundation's Matt McClain, "a cathartic moment of validation."[4] Although the Save Trestles battle is not over, learning from the victory at Del Mar will be a critical step in the process to help preserve other endangered waves in California and globally.

Surfers Can't Fight Alone

The biggest lesson from Del Mar is that surfers cannot fight coastal battles on their own. While the Surfrider Foundation did a brilliant job of mobilizing the masses and creating the coolest marketing campaign in the history of the environmental movement, the Save Trestles coalition included the best and brightest of California's environmental community. The Sierra Club, through the Friends of the Foothills, used the best tactics of grassroots organizing and social marketing to get the public to take action. The environmental organization also organized key advocacy trips to Sacramento for grassroots campaigners. The Natural Resources Defense Council, Endangered Habitats League, San Onofre Foundation, Wildcoast, California Coastal Protection Network, California State Parks Foundation, the City Project, and a host of other organizations and consultants also provided the political, legal, and organizing savvy to help convince the coastal commission to derail the toll road. This was as sophisticated an environmental coalition and campaign as I have ever seen.

To save other endangered waves, we have to build equally strong teams that include birdwatchers, biologists, and lawyers. We have to connect endangered waves to the communities who cherish the watersheds that gave them life. Most important is that we have to do what McClain calls "building our army one person at a time." "During the Trestle campaign," McClain told me, "each time we brought someone into the fold, they ended up bringing a few of their friends with them. Next thing you know, we have an army."

Pro Surfing Is about Leadership

With the exception of mountain climbing and river kayaking, there is no other professional sport as dependent on natural ecosystems as surfing. If there were no reef, there would be no Pipeline in Oahu; no shoreline, no Jeffrey's Bay in South Africa; no San Mateo Creek watershed, no Trestles. This means that more than any other group of professional athletes, surfers have an obligation to defend the surf breaks that make their livelihoods possible.

During the Save Trestles campaign, a large group of pro surfers defended San Onofre State Beach. Pat O'Connell, a star of *Endless Summer II* and Fuel TV's *Drive Thru* series, lent his time and cheerful personality to the cause. Taylor Knox, a surf tour veteran, also helped the Surfrider Foundation lobby hard for Trestles early on.

As I walked into the Del Mar "pit" just outside Wyland Hall on Big Wednesday, I felt as if I were at the Action Sport Retail Expo or the Surf Industry's annual Waterman's Ball environmental fundraiser. Big-wave surfers Greg and Rusty Long walked up with their dad, Steve, the San Onofre State Beach superintendent and founder of the San Onofre Foundation. Surf tour veterans Damien and C. J. Hobgood signed autographs for eager young surfers.

Australian pro surfing pioneer and former world surfing champion Peter Townend wandered in and out of the crowd. California surfing pioneers Mickey Muñoz and Woody Eckstrom greeted longtime friends. Inside the arena, surfing statesmen and former world surfing champion Shaun Tomson planted himself directly in front of the commissioners to make sure they did the right thing.

While the graceful and athletic surfing of Pat, Taylor, Rusty, Greg, Damien, C. J., Shaun, and their colleagues inspires me, I was even more thrilled by their leadership. With more young surfers than ever dreaming of life in the pro surfing fast lane, their elders on the pro tour and those retired from it need to mentor young surfers in the art of giving back to our sport by selflessly helping to protect the waves that sustain our sport.

Real Locals Save Waves

I was a little worried when I was first invited to be a part of the Save Trestles Coalition. I imagined that hardcore Trestles surfers might not be too happy about an Imperial Beach local speaking out publicly about preserving their treasured spot. Instead, the opposite happened. The threat of the toll road created a steadfast community of longtime locals and California surfers alike who recognize what a special place Trestles is, whether they surf it every day or just a few times a year. More important is that when I walk down that trail with my two sons during what for them are pilgrimages (my sons celebrate their birthdays surfing Trestles with their friends), I see more smiles and watch more wildlife than at any other spot I surf in Southern California.

So this is the message for the grumpy surfers who embody localism and are obsessed with keeping outsiders from enjoying "their" spot—do not expect us to lift a finger when the bulldozers start dropping rocks into the lineup of your "personal" beach. At Bell's Beach, one of Australia's most iconic surf spots, local surfers and environmentalists have built national alliances to stop housing development projects that they believe would ruin the aesthetic quality and the ecological integrity of their Surfing Recreation Reserve. The tradeoff for increased crowds at Bell's is the preservation of the understated beauty of one of the world's most unique surfing areas. It is our job as coastal stewards to safeguard our tribal gathering spots against physical destruction for future generations.

Sharing waves with your neighbors will create an army ready to defend your break at a moment's notice.

Cultural Diversity Counts

One of the best-received arguments made to the coastal commissioners was that obliterating San Mateo Campground and San Onofre State Beach was an issue of environmental health and justice. The recreational users of San Onofre State Beach are among the most culturally diverse of any coastal state park in California. On any given day in the state park, you can talk surfboard design with Asian American surfers, admire the grace of local multicultural cross-country high school running teams traversing the park's trails, marvel at the prowess of some of the world's best Hispanic surfers, and according to Pat Zabrocki, "listen to conversations in about four different languages."

At the commission hearing, Los Angeles civil rights and environmental attorney Robert Garcia and Acjachemen tribal activist Rebecca Robles and other Native American leaders provided a moving and passionate defense of San Onofre as a critical site for providing access to open space and as a recreational and cultural resource for underserved communities. The San Mateo Creek watershed is actually Panhe, a key Acjachemen religious, historical, and ceremonial site.

The involvement of Latino, African American, Asian–Pacific Islander, and Native American organizations in the Save Trestles movement underscores the need for environmentalists, the surf industry, and surfers to expand our efforts to reach out to underserved communities and people of color. This is not only an issue of tactics and strategy but also a moral and ethical imperative that will help us reclaim the heart and soul of surfing and revitalize the environmental movement.

The Rise of the Surf Industry

The multibillion-dollar surf industry is relatively young and just starting to flex its political muscles. The industry was an active participant in the Save Trestles campaign and was out in full force in Del Mar. During lunch, I said hello to surf industry veterans including Paul Naude of Billabong, Sean Smith of the Surf Industry Manufacturing Association (SIMA), Dick Baker of OP, Gary Ward of Ocean Minded, and surf industry veteran Bob Mignogna. Later in the afternoon, Baker spoke to the commission about the economic value of Trestles and the importance of the multibillion-dollar surfing industry to the economy of California.

The surf media also played a critical role in building up the Save Trestles movement and keeping people informed about the latest developments. Just before the commission hearing, the Surfrider Foundation posted before-and-after toll road images on Surfline.com and Surfermag .com. The postings hit the surfing world like a bomb. The photos illustrated how the toll toad would obliterate San Mateo Creek. They also convinced the surf community what was at stake and the need to attend the Del Mar hearing.

Surf industry and media involvement in the Save Trestles campaign was a very positive and welcome sign for the future of the coastal protection movement in California and worldwide. "The whole Trestles event and hearing made it very clear that the industry as a whole realizes environmental battles are not just about writing a check or getting others involved," Sean Smith of SIMA told me. "This is a collective effort and everyone needs to get and stay involved. That day was not just about an individual brand or company. We were all there to make sure that Trestles didn't get plowed over by a toll road."

Real Surfers Can Be Politicians

During the afternoon of Big Wednesday, meeting attendees were treated to a political spectacle as hypocritical and fake as any congressional committee hearing in Washington. "The TCA loaded the dais with various Orange County city councilmen and women, most of who conveniently sit on the TCA Board," wrote Matt McClain. "In a mind-numbing marathon-like drone that could only be compared to a congressional filibuster, the officials spoke . . . and spoke . . . and spoke, repeating one another's tired party line ad nauseam. Sitting in the crowd, you could literally see the Commissioners' eyes glazing over."[5]

Our communities can no longer afford to be represented by elected officials who call themselves surfers for political gain. We need real surfers—men and women who live and breathe for the taste of saltwater and the thrill of a new northwest swell—to run for office. But they have to be the kind of individuals who understand that being a surfer is first and foremost always about riding *and* preserving waves and beaches.

Being a real surfer means defending your spot against development and ruination—whatever the cost.

The battle over Trestles and against the toll road is far from over. The TCA will take its case to the U.S. Department of Commerce and try every trick in the book to pave over the San Mateo Creek watershed. But the decisive nature of the coastal commission call proves that in California, messing with our state parks and surf spots is a bad idea. It also showed that surfers have finally accepted our role as defenders of our tribal homeland—the California coastline—for generations to come.

23

Saving Trestles, Part III

Rumble in Del Mar

After the decision by the California Coastal Commission to deny the TCA a coastal development permit, the transportation agency appealed to the U.S. Department of Commerce. The federal government was the final "decider" because land for San Onofre State Beach is leased from the federal government. After receiving more than thirty thousand e-mails and letters asking for a public hearing on the issue to be held in Southern California, the federal agency, headed by Commerce Secretary Carlos Gutierrez (a former Kellogg Company CEO), agreed to hold a hearing at the Bren Center on the campus of the University of California–Irvine on July 25, 2008.

The center had a capacity of 4,758, more than enough to seat what activists expected to be a crowd of between 3,500 and 4,000. But UC–Irvine officials cancelled the event. They believed that the more than 10,000 people predicted to attend the toll road hearing would have exceeded the center's capacity. Rather than quickly identify a new location for the hearing, the Commerce Department argued that it did not have the budget to accommodate a larger facility.

The Save San Onofre Coalition and the State of California urged the U.S. Department of Commerce to schedule a new public hearing. Jamee Jordan Patterson of the California Attorney General's office requested that the federal agency hold a meeting at the Del Mar Fairgrounds during the second week of September. Once again, surfers and environmentalists flooded Gutierrez with e-mails and phone calls urging the Commerce Department to hold a new hearing. Gutierrez agreed once again to hold the hearing at the Del Mar Fairgrounds.

On the morning of September 22, I entered the cavernous livestock exhibition hall at the Del Mar Fairgrounds. The atmosphere at Del Mar II was much different from the festive party atmosphere of the California Coastal Commission hearing seven months earlier. The second hearing was tightly controlled and designed to eliminate any type of party atmosphere. Security guards controlled the crowd, restricting signs and demonstrations. Booths for environmental groups were kept away from the main hall. The hearing was not as much fun as its predecessor.

Jane Luxton (general counsel for the National Oceanic and Atmospheric Administration [NOAA], administered by the Commerce Department) presided over the hearing. Luxton called up speakers, enforced an arcane list of bizarre rules, and maintained a waxy smile for more than ten hours of public testimony. Red-shirted private security guards enforced the rules and threatened to eject my two sons for carrying a homemade sign that was apparently a few inches too large. Two anonymous aides shared the dais with Luxton. This almost surreal atmosphere caused Surfrider Foundation CEO Jim Moriarty to tell me as we took a midday fresh air break, "I just hope they don't put the testimony into a report somewhere and make the decision they already planned on making."

My doubts about the process were reinforced by my presentation to Luxton and the NOAA panel. I asked seven young surfers from Imperial Beach to accompany me to the speaker podium to demonstrate the importance of preserving San Onofre State Beach as an open space for children. While we were gathering in the speaker staging area to the right of the podium, an agitated security guard informed me that the children were forbidden. I informed him that NOAA officials had approved their presence. The guard ignored me and ordered the children to stand down.

After I politely declined the guard's request, he rushed over to NOAA officials on the sidelines and argued that I was in violation of rules he had invented at that very moment. NOAA staff calmed him down, and I was able to speak to Luxton and her panel while the young surfers stood silently behind me.

Given the thousands of people who showed up to oppose the toll road plan at Del Mar II, it would be difficult for Gutierrez to overturn the California Coastal Commission's rejection of the plan. I can only hope that the commerce secretary leaves the tattered blueprints for the toll road in a desk drawer in an empty office in Washington, D.C., after President Bush departs for Texas.

On December 19, 2008, the U.S. Department of Commerce denied the TCA's request to overturn the California Coastal Commission's rejection of the toll road, effectively killing the project. The TCA is seeking to restart the toll road project again.

24

Surfing Can Change the World

O n any given day in the lineup in Imperial Beach, Baltazar Macías, an athletic and determined surfer who grew up in Playas de Tijuana, is one of a select group of hardcore locals aggressively riding whatever wave comes his way. Whether a wave is small, big, mediocre, or epic, Baltazar chooses his line and makes his move. He is a man with a plan.

But surfing in Imperial Beach is not easy. In 2009, a year with almost no rain, the Boca Rio, famed for board-crushing barrels, was closed for over one hundred days due to pollution from Mexico. The Imperial Beach pier, a spot that can absolutely rock on a south swell, with roping wedging lefts spitting out of its north side, was closed for more than eighteen days. To make matters worse, beach closures that were once just a winter problem caused by the rain-swollen and sewage-filled Tijuana River now also occur during the spring, summer, and fall. South swells and wind push sewage north to Imperial Beach from Playas de Tijuana and Punta Banderas discharges. During south swells, the sweet chemical stench of sewage often hangs over the Imperial Beach beachfront.

For Baltazar, the reality of Imperial Beach does not diminish his faith in the power of surfing to change our destiny and create an alternative future. With that manifesto of hope, Baltazar brought the First Annual Bad Boy Pro-Am to the south side of the Imperial Beach pier with a couple thousand bucks in prize money.

A surf contest is not revolutionary—except when it is. As much as Imperial Beach has problems, it is an oasis of peace in a border region filled with poverty and violence. Walls, not waves, divide surfers who ride the same swells, suffer from the same pollution, and cross the artificial border both ways in search of clean waves.

To wipe out the boundaries that divide us, Baltazar invited pros from Mexico to cross the border, summoned members of the Japanese Surfing Association, and reached out to talented but cash-poor surfers from the U.S.–Mexico border to Oceanside. "I wanted to create an event that everyone can afford," Baltazar said after a morning surf session in

A beach closure sign at Imperial Beach in California.

Imperial Beach. "It was important to invite people up from Mexico to participate in a positive event that brings people together."

Baltazar's optimism, determination, and belief in the power of surfing to make the world a better place is what inspires me to continue battling to stop the worldwide push to replace our remaining wild coastline with marinas, toll roads, and breakwaters. There is nothing more beautiful and more satisfying on earth than a good day of surfing. And we have no future unless we forever preserve the beaches, waves, and oceans that sustain us.

Epilogue

Reclaiming the Coast

My drive through the Ensenada–Tijuana coastal corridor (described in the opening chapter) was preceded by a four-day 190-mile off-road and off-the-grid drive down the Pacific coastline of central Baja California. Finding Punta Canoas, a remote headland, required a drive down a 60-mile dusty, meandering dirt track that veers off the Transpeninsular Highway blacktop about 40 miles south of the farming village of El Rosario. The dirt road passes through verdant cardon cactus and boojum forests followed by a descent into one of Baja's most notorious badlands.

My Wildcoast colleagues Saul Alarcon and Zach Plopper marked our progress on two GPS-enabled Xplore Tablet PCs against a previous track made the year before. Despite the plethora of navigational hardware, I took the wrong turn into an arroyo that ended up at a beach that offered up a panorama of miles of fortress cliffs to the north, blue-gray whitecapped sea, and washed-out sky. After a quick lunch, we backtracked south through meandering moonlike gullies and after an hour arrived at our destination—a salt marsh hidden between two jutting headlands capped by sandstone spires with a cobble coastline and a garbage-strewn fish camp.

The protected beach inside the northern headland, now occupied by the fish camp, had been the proposed site of a Nautical Ladder marina. After pitching our tents in a sandpit protected from the wind by a large tamarisk tree and a cobblestone berm, we made a campfire and watched the full moon rise into the nighttime desert sky.

During the next three days, we surveyed just about every beach, point, and wetland for 130 miles along the Pacific. Over the course of our four-day coastal transect, the only signs of civilization were occasional solitary fish camps. We stopped to talk to hermitlike ranchers and fishermen encountered along the way. Wildlife was abundant. A mule deer ran into a cactus forest as we emerged from a lush mountain pass. Fat coyotes played a game of hide-and-seek as we sped through mud flats. A large female peregrine falcon guarded her nest perched atop a craggy point overlooking miles of desert coastline and salt marsh.[1]

The view from Punta Canoas.

The stretch of Cirios coastline with its wildlife, empty beaches, and pristine point waves was a microcosm of everything that the mythical wild Baja has come to mean and everything that was almost lost during the Baja Boom years. Luckily, by the time of the trip, in March 2009, the Nautical Ladder marina project and just about every other scheme—the entire Baja boom, LNG terminals (with the exception of the Sempra Energy Costa Azul project in northern Baja), the Loreto Bay resort, Bajagua, the TCA toll road, and plans to remove seals from a tiny La Jolla beach—had collapsed. They were buried under their own morass of obsolescence and irrelevance in the face of the new swell of reality: global economic recession, the elections of President Obama in the United States and Felipe Calderón in Mexico, the return to a more rational resource management policy in both countries, and the specter of global climate change and sea-level rise.

However, the fact that the economic and political reality of coastal conservation and development has changed has not always reached the ears of the minor functionaries, coastal lobbyists, and elected officials desperate for shovel-ready projects to please their developer and labor constituents. In Mexico, many government planners and powerful politicians still cling to dreams of *macro-proyectos* that are a throwback to the era of PRI-style Sovietlike central planning. In the United States, officials use federal funds to support bad coastal projects that are a throwback to 1950s-style engineering boondoggles.

That is not to say that the conservationists and coastal advocates did not make a difference in stopping these projects. They did. Therefore, it is critical to review these campaigns and the status of the projects discussed in this book to help identify lessons learned.

Baja California: A Return to the Wild

The battle over Mitsubishi's planned salt project in San Ignacio Lagoon did more than anything that took place before or after for efforts to spur the conservation movement in the Baja California peninsula and to preserve the lagoon itself. Since the project was stopped in 2000, Wildcoast and our partners in the Laguna San Ignacio Conservation Alliance have carried out the following: preserved coastal habitat owned by ejidos; facilitated a micro-credit loan program to switch fishing and whale-watching two-stroke outboard engines to less-polluting and more-fuel-efficient four-stroke engines; and partnered with the National Natural Protected Area Commission of Mexico (CONANP) to designate federally owned lagoon habitat as conservation lands. Although a paved highway now under construction from the inland village of San Ignacio could open up the lagoon to further incremental urban development, the alliance is also supporting an effort to implement the first-ever lagoon urban land-use plan in partnership with the County of Mulegé.

However, changes brought on by global climate change do not bode well for the lagoon and its gray whales. Research on the phenomenon of "skinny whales," or gray whales without sufficient food, is ongoing. Scientists are attempting to determine whether the gray whale population has been and will be significantly affected by a decline of amphipods, their primary food source, in northern feeding grounds, related to an increase in average sea temperature. Any decline in the gray whale population could have a significant impact on lagoon residents who supplement their meager fishing income with the more lucrative whale-watching business.[2]

My Los Cirios coast transect ended at the half-built and abandoned marina in the fishing village of Santa Rosalillita. The modern glass-and-steel complex includes a port captain's office, an empty Pemex gas station, a row of storage garages, and two rock jetties jutting into the surf that are now partially buried by sand. In fact, so much sand has built up around the jetties that the marina has been transformed into a surf spot during North Pacific swells.

That Santa Rosalillita was the worst location to build a marina on the entire Pacific coast of Baja California was obvious to anyone with experience observing waves and beaches. FONATUR officials had anticipated more than two dozen similar marinas throughout Mexico under the Nautical Ladder plan. However, FONATUR overestimated demand for its anticipated marina slips by 600 percent.[3] But McCarthy's marina development project began its decline when Wildcoast helped put his plan under the glare of a June 11, 2003, feature story in the *Wall Street Journal* that observed, "Cancun would be hard to duplicate anywhere, much less along the craggy, desolate Baja coast."

The day the article appeared, I debated McCarthy on Mexico's Radio Imagen during the very popular morning national news and talk show hosted by Pedro Ferriz de Con. During our debate, McCarthy announced that FONATUR would scale back its plans for Pacific coast marinas.

Meanwhile, a coalition of Mexican conservationists led by the Mexican Biodiversity Fund's Lorenzo Rosensweig negotiated directly with FONATUR and the Mexican Environment Ministry to induce them to scale back project plans even further. Even Carlos Slim, Mexico's richest man, lent his yacht to host a meeting of behind-the-scenes negotiations between conservationists and government officials seeking a more modest tourism investment project targeted at improving Mexico's existing marina infrastructure rather than building new marinas in the desert.

In 2007, Wildcoast arranged a meeting at the San Diego Natural History Museum between Mexico's tourism minister, Rodolfo Elizondo Torres, and conservationist critics of the FONATUR marina plan. Elizondo seemed to be searching for a face-saving way of finally killing the Nautical Ladder. Soon after the meeting, Elizondo officially terminated the marina plan.

The Nautical Ladder's chief proponent, John McCarthy, was the subject of an investigation by a Mexican congressional committee that concluded that the former time-share salesman "had neither the technical [n]or political capacity to carry out the Nautical Ladder project despite having spent more than 1.5 billion pesos ($150 million dollars), an embarrassing situation that gives Mexico a bad international image."[4] Rumors abound about McCarthy's current involvement in promoting dubious development projects in the East Cape.

The biggest eyesores in the Baja California peninsula are the high-rise remnants of the Baja Boom turned bust that are spread out between Tijuana and Ensenada. Without a hint of irony, realtors refer to the region as the "Gold Coast." With more than two dozen abandoned high-rise condo and hotel projects as of February 2010, however, this tarnished coast would more accurately be called the "Ghost Town Coast."

Given the dubious nature of much of the development and the lack of any attempt by builders to execute plans with any sense of scale that fits the local landscape, it is more than likely that once the economy revives, developers will bring back their construction crews to operate the tower cranes that now sit idle. There is also speculation that large desalination plants could be built along the coastline to provide water for even more badly planned development in Baja California.[5]

The state government of Baja California is still attempting to revive the proposed megaport project and new industrial city of Puerto Colonet south of Ensenada. The planned port project could become the behemoth that completely transforms patterns of land development in one of the peninsula's most biologically important areas.[6] Despite what has been the encroaching agricultural frontier of the San Quintín Valley, the Colonet region still contains almost extinct coastal vernal pools and globally rare coastal chaparral habitat. Extensive pine-oak forests inhabited by mountain lions and California condors can be found in the Sierra San Pedro Martir to the east. With the promise of a new industrial port and city at Punta Colonet, it is quite likely that the Gold Coast mess could be extended another hundred miles south of Ensenada.

There is speculation that if the PRI returns to power in 2012 during the next presidential elections, it will be through the machinations of the murky and ultraconservative Grupo de Atlacomulco. That shadowy group based out of the state of Mexico appears to be promoting a new economic development plan based on *macro-proyectos*, huge infrastructure projects that would more than likely involve paving over natural areas and coastlines throughout Mexico.

The only apparent lesson that government officials and their developer partners have learned from the collapse of the Gold Coast is that the trail of failed development projects throughout Baja California were not grandiose enough. In late 2009, developers dredged an estuary adjacent to the East Cape village of La Ribera and dumped boulders in the surf zone to serve as jetties for a future marina. Soon after, the Santa Rosalillita scenario played out again there, and sand began to fill in between the jetties. Not too far away, Hansa Urbana, a Spanish resort and real estate company, is planning a massive golf course and marina development near the fragile Cabo Pulmo coral reef. Other planned projects in the East Cape promise to transform this delicate coastal region into the next coastal playground of the ultrawealthy.

The coastal ruin along the Gold Coast, hyperdevelopment in celebrity-filled Los Cabos, and planned development in the East Cape give greater impetus for conservationists to preserve the remaining stretches of wild coastline remaining in the Baja California peninsula. To counter such development, organizations such as Wildcoast, Niparajá, The Nature Conservancy, Terra Peninsular, the International Community Foundation, and Pronatura Noroeste used the land conservation model established in San Ignacio Lagoon to further conservation endeavors with coastal ejidos throughout the peninsula. Now there are efforts to permanently preserve ecologically sensitive coastal habitats through land acquisition and conservation easements in the Loreto–La Paz corridor, Bahía Concepción, Magdalena Bay, Bahía de los Angeles, and the Los Cirios Pacific Coast region. Building the capacity of environmentalists in Mexico who can help make good conservation deals and are not afraid to openly confront government agencies and private developers in order to shut down illegal development in wild areas is more important than ever.

As a response to the Escalera Nautica and other badly planned coastal development projects, CONANP also dramatically expanded its efforts to preserve the federal maritime coastal zone (sixty feet above the mean high-tide line) and unassigned federal coastal lands as conservation areas throughout the federal protected areas of Baja California. This unprecedented policy initiative comes from the frustration of CONANP from having to fight off development threats such as the Nautical Ladder and the Mitsubishi salt project that should never have been proposed in the first place, because of their location in what are supposed to be off-limits federal protected areas.

In addition, the ongoing and escalating Mexican drug war has had a significant impact on life in Baja California and the capacity of Mexican officials to attract tourists to enjoy the natural wonders of the peninsula. With over 28,000 drug-related deaths in Mexico since President Calderon took office in December 2006 and the drug-war-related deaths of more than 200 Americans since 2004, tourism to Baja has plummeted. The muted and delayed response by the Mexican government to a string of attacks in northern Baja California on American surfers and Baja 1000 off-road race crew members in late 2007 further curtailed tourism to Baja California. Federal and state tourism officials have not been able to reconcile their desire for mass tourism with the reality of narco-war violence, robberies, and shootouts in Tijuana and Rosarito Beach. In theory, the plethora of ski-masked and armed soldiers in pickups equipped with mounted machine guns should make tourists feel safer. For many tourists, however, the repeated military checkpoints, combined with the garbage and graffiti that plague Baja's large and small cities, only reinforce the sense of insecurity and danger.

Despite the threats to Baja California's coastline and the drug war, the capacity of conservation organizations is greater than at any time in Mexico's modern history. In 1993, when I first learned of the Mitsubishi salt project, there were only a handful of organizations in Mexico with the capacity to challenge the project. Now there are well-established environmental networks and independent activists operating throughout the peninsula and in Mexico with strong links to international organizations. What is missing is the existence of a sophisticated network of organizations and activists who can effectively advocate in Mexico City with the increasingly independent Mexican Congress and influence the once-imperial Mexican presidency. Organizations have to relearn how to work with and against the government to protect the coast. Environmentalists also need to seek out and partner with emerging green leaders in Mexico's private sector.

More critically, Mexico's environmentalists must lose their fear of angering powerful politicians by opposing illegal projects. They cannot be afraid to overtly and publicly use their political power to challenge corruption and the destruction of Mexico's natural heritage. There is too much at stake because their biggest challenge will be to strategically and permanently preserve the ecological integrity and biodiversity of the pristine bays, lagoons, islands, and beaches of Baja California and the Sea of Cortez. On this issue there must be a permanent line in the sand.

The U.S.–Mexico Border: Recovery and Restoration

By the end of the Bush administration in January 2009, two attempts to contain terrorism had been launched along the U.S.–Mexico border. The progress of both could be viewed from the hillside straddling Smuggler's Gulch. On the Mexican side of the fence, soldiers wearing battle fatigues and carrying machine guns searched vehicles along the highway as part of Mexico's war on narco-terrorists.

On the U.S. side of the gulch, construction crews applied the finishing touches to the earthen, concrete, and metal border barrier. The barrier was designed to defend Americans from Islamic jihadists. It will have no impact on the Mexican drug lords financed by U.S. narcotics sales who kill Mexican soldiers and citizens with weapons purchased in America. The inability of the two nations to deal with their intersection of geography has resulted in the erosion of democracy. Meanwhile, the flow of polluted air and water across the border continues.

The imposition of a national security state along the U.S. side of the border was much more dramatic than in Mexico. The Department of Homeland Security enacted draconian security measures to prevent U.S. citizens from viewing its Maginot Line–inspired engineering and security masterwork along the border. Meanwhile, the staff of the Tijuana River Reserve, part of the National Estuarine Research Reserve system, negotiated with Homeland Security officials the terms of managing a federally protected fragile salt coastal estuary within a war zone. The contradictions between conflict and conservation along the U.S.–Mexico border reached their height as government agencies came to terms with each other over rights to protect and interact with nature.

For the Tijuana Estuary staff and conservationists, the only solution to the lack of democracy on the border was to convince the Obama administration to mitigate the damage already done by the former Bush administration's border barrier. But that effort mattered little after a massive rainstorm hit the region, causing mudslides that partially buried a salt marsh, ranches, and farms in the Tijuana River valley. There is no happy ending here. The damage caused by the Department of Homeland Security's border barrier harmed the rule of law, wildlife, and an ecosystem shared by Mexico and the United States at great cost to the U.S. Treasury. The Government Accountability Office estimated that the upkeep of the new barrier along the U.S.–Mexico border would cost an estimated $6.5 billion over the next twenty years.[7]

The effort by Bajagua to win a $600 million federal sole-source, no-bid contract to build a sewage treatment plant in Tijuana was halted by the International Boundary and Water Commission on May 15, 2008. The intervention of Senator Dianne Feinstein in the effort played a crucial role in stopping the Bajagua project. The result was a complete resuscitation of governmental efforts to deal with binational water pollution and trash flows. The demise of Bajagua also resulted in the construction of a new secondary sewage treatment plant on the U.S. side of the border,

A pile of flood debris in the U.S. side of the Tijuana River valley.

saving American taxpayers an estimated $200 million over the cost of the now-defunct Bajagua scheme.

After the cancellation of the Bajagua project, the State of California's Water Quality Control Board convened a multiagency task force to deal with increasing sewage, sediment, and trash flows across the border. Environmental organizations also convened a binational coalition to pressure government agencies to develop a comprehensive plan to deal with transboundary water pollution.

Three new small-scale sewage treatment plants have been placed online in the Tijuana–Rosarito Beach region. To treat Mexican sewage, constructing and operating smaller treatment plants in Tijuana is cheaper than building expensive large sewage treatment plants north of the border. There is also a major effort under way to reclaim and reuse Tijuana's wastewater, a pioneering effort in Mexico.[8]

Additionally, the private sector has to take a more active leadership role in tackling Tijuana's growing urban crisis. So far, the only action in this regard taken by Tijuana's elite has been to flee the city for the wealthy suburbs of San Diego. Reducing cross-border water and air pollution will occur only if we can reframe environmental issues as about improving the quality of life for families in Tijuana. Until having neighborhoods awash in untreated sewage and garbage piling up around Tijuana is considered an outrage, the problem of cross-border sewage flows will never be resolved.

The campaign to halt Chevron-Texaco's proposed LNG terminal adjacent to the Coronado Islands came to an end in March 2007, when the company killed the project because of a combination of factors, including competition from the Sempra Energy plant at Costa Azul, a complaint filed against the project filed with the NAFTA-related Commission for Environmental Cooperation in Montreal by environmentalists (including Wildcoast), and the fact that the market for imported natural gas has lessened considerably since the project's conception. Bill Powers, the activist who helped lead the effort to repel the multiple LNG projects proposed for the Californias, repeatedly stated during our meetings with LNG project proponents that because of the large supply of domestic natural gas, imported LNG was absolutely unnecessary. What had been almost a dozen proposals to build either portside or offshore LNG terminals in Baja California and California had by May 2009 been reduced to three in Southern California. However, oil and gas companies moved their plans to build LNG terminals from the Californias to Oregon (four planned), British Columbia in Canada (three planned) and Sonora in Mexico (one planned). With the volatile international energy market more in flux than ever and the promise of a green energy revolution on the horizon, whether these outdated projects will come to fruition remains to be seen.

The U.S.–Mexico border can no longer be a no-man's-land that provides refuge for corporations seeking to escape U.S. environmental laws and elected officials seeking to blame Mexican migrants for our nation's problems. Oscar Romo, a longtime environmental advocate in Tijuana who now works for the Tijuana River National Estuarine Research Reserve, said to me one sunny afternoon outside the reserve's Visitor Center in Imperial Beach, "We have to look at this area not as being binational because that only creates a division. We are one region. The more we think that way, the easier it will be to help solve our problems."

Southern California: Back to Basics

In Southern California, political change and budget crisis dramatically transformed the coastal conservation landscape by reducing the market and finances for coastal development. Unfortunately, the salient obstacle to coastal protection in Southern California is the lucrative potential profit of even small construction projects, which enables developers to engage an army of lobbyists, lawyers, and elected officials to advocate on their behalf. This makes it harder for ordinary coastal community residents or grassroots groups to fight projects without the assistance of larger environmental organizations that have the expertise and full-time staff to give them the capacity to push back.

The irrational effort by the City of San Diego to remove a small population of harbor seals came to a conclusion with the arrival of a new city council and a budget crisis. By 2009, San Diego city officials had become reluctant to spend over a million dollars to dredge a tiny beach in the relatively affluent community of La Jolla when swimming pools and recreation centers in low-income neighborhoods were being closed or cut back. A new state law authored by California state senator Christine Kehoe amended a 1931 trust that identified the seal beach as an area only for children, to permit its use as a marine mammal habitat.

Protecting harbor seals in La Jolla has national implications because sea otters, once sequestered north of Point Conception, are slowly moving south. It is not unreasonable to assume that these once nearly extinct marine mammals will soon be cavorting in the kelp beds and reefs of Southern California, including La Jolla.[9] Conserving marine mammal populations in densely populated urban coastal areas in Southern California is a national test case for our ability to protect coastal and marine ecosystems and the wildlife they harbor.

In California, the concern over the proliferation of LNG terminals had shifted to alarm over the prospect of offshore oil drilling. What had been an attempt at the end of the Bush administration to fast-track new oil drilling off the California coast changed considerably with the arrival of the Obama administration. One of the first major policy initiatives of Interior Secretary Ken Salazar was to hold a public hearing in San Francisco on April 16, 2009, to engage public input on the issue. Most of the more than a thousand people who attended supported continuing the drilling ban. Prominent elected officials including Senator Barbara Boxer all spoke out against renewed drilling.

In the aftermath of the British Petroleum Deepwater Horizon oil spill, the issue of offshore oil drilling will not disappear. Offshore oil drilling and especially deepwater drilling represent the most significant threat to the coastlines of California and North America. Protecting our coastal and marine ecosystems against future oil spills will require heavy federal regulation of the oil industry, a permanent ban on deepwater drilling and offshore drilling in sensitive areas, and serious investment in the clean and green energy and technology industries rather than the antiquated oil business.

In the most surprising but welcome development of all, on December 19, 2008, the U.S. Department of Commerce denied the Transportation Corridor Agencies' appeal of the California Coastal Commission's rejection of the Foothill South, or San Onofre–Trestles, toll road project. The action by then–commerce secretary Carlos Gutierrez surprised many anti-toll activists. But thanks to their efforts, the Save Trestles campaign was arguably one of the most effective environmental campaigns in California history. Despite the TCA's initial first-round loss, the agency is continuing its lobbying efforts in an attempt to obtain federal support to resurrect the toll road project in a new form.

While the Save Trestles campaign and victory was a watershed in the organizing capacity of the environmental movement in California, many activists questioned whether they would have to mount similar campaigns for every effort to preserve threatened open space in Southern California. That is why, to prevent future development projects from threatening state parks, the California State Parks Foundation sponsored state legislation preventing the use of state parks for corporate or private use.

With the threat of global climate change looming, environmentalists are going to have to be more proactive about preserving the remaining coastal open space and natural coastal and marine ecosystems that remain in California. One example of this has been the effort to develop a system of marine protected areas (MPAs) off the California coast. Faced with rancorous pushback by backward-looking commercial and sport-fishing interests, conservationists settled for a proposal for a modified network of MPAs that are at least a start to conserving and restoring critical marine habitats and fish spawning sites in California.

However, wily coastal lobbyists, developers, and government officials have managed to green-wash many of their new coastal projects. Proponents of antiquated desalination plants, for example, have painted their projects as a sensible way of dealing with California's ongoing drought problem. Despite the massive energy needs (which some activists believed were the reason behind Southern California LNG proposals) of such projects, the California Coastal Commission gave final approval for Poseidon Resources to build a massive desalination plant in Carlsbad,

California. Efforts to build these plants instead of investing in water conservation represent a new global threat to coastal and marine resources. Desalination projects are planned and threaten the coast in California, Baja California, and Australia.[10]

To stem the tide of projected sea-level rise and to stop coastal erosion, agencies such as the U.S. Army Corps of Engineers have proposed spending hundreds of millions of dollars carrying out sand replenishment projects in Southern California. These projects cause massive damage to sensitive coastal and marine ecosystems and wildlife, especially fisheries resources. They should not be an alternative to the much more cost-effective and long policy of coastal retreat, dam removal, and wetland and watershed restoration that could help revitalize coastal resources rather than destroy them, as in the case of sand replenishment.[11]

Unfortunately, coastal protection campaigns require an incredibly sophisticated level of political advocacy, fundraising, coalition building, and media-savviness that cannot always be replicated in every campaign. That is why the energy we gain from being in the ocean and the everyday world we live in must be the driving force behind campaigns to preserve our natural heritage and coastal lifestyle. But these battles can no longer just be fought by white upper-middle-class coastal dwellers. Environmentalists have to reach out to the entire spectrum of culturally and economically diverse Americans. If we are to build an environmental movement that is sustainable, we need to help foster a new generation of environmental leaders among African American, Latino, Native American, and Asian–Pacific Islander communities and link open-space conservation with community health and renewal.

In this climate change–threatened twenty-first century, being blue and green needs to be cool, hip, strategically brilliant, and targeted at building a culturally and economically diverse movement to help restore degraded coastal watersheds and preserve every inch of natural coastline and wild ocean spaces we have left. Activism by battle-ready conservationists will always be necessary, because somewhere, someplace, there will always be a corporation or government agency poised to destroy world-class beaches, wetlands, lagoons, islands, and the wildlife that thrive there. They will not negotiate, compromise, or mitigate their impact. And no matter whether it is in the United States or Mexico, an army of activists and coastal residents will have to battle the pirates who would destroy the last refuge and escape we have—our wild sea.

Glossary

A-frame. Type of wave characterized by a peak that can be ridden in both left and right directions.

Arroyo. A gully cut by an intermittent stream.

Baja Boom. The period from about 1995 through 2008 when development dramatically increased in the Baja California peninsula, especially in the Tijuana–Ensenada coastal corridor, the Cape Region, and south of Loreto.

Bajagua. A company based in San Diego that proposed the construction of a U.S.-taxpayer-subsidized private-sector sewage treatment plant in eastern Tijuana.

Barrel. The hollow part of a wave that a surfer can ride inside.

Beachbreak. A surf break that occurs over a beach with sand.

Bottom turn. A surfing movement that involves making a sharp turn at the bottom of the wave to set up for an upcoming maneuver.

Bowl. A part of a wave characterized by significant hollowness and wedge.

Caguama. Pronounced *ca-wa-ma*, this term for "sea turtle" in Baja California can refer to all types of sea turtles or specifically to East Pacific green sea turtles or loggerhead turtles (alternatively, to a large bottle of Pacifico beer favored by fishermen), depending on the location.

Colonia. The term for a neighborhood or district in Mexico; it can also refer to an informal urban settlement.

Cutback. A maneuver in surfing in which a rider turns back from the outer part of the wave to the part of the wave closer to the curl.

Dawn patrol. A predawn outing by surfers to catch waves at first light during optimal conditions.

Duende. A fairy- or goblinlike creature. In Magdalena Bay, many fishermen believe in the existence of a race of duendes that live in hillside caves on Magdalena Island.

Ejido. A communal system of landownership in Mexico. While typically ejidos consist of agricultural land, ejidos in the Baja California peninsula often include large tracts of desert used for grazing and ranching.

Escalera Nautica. In 2001, the National Tourism Fund of Mexico proposed the development of a system of marinas, or a "Nautical Ladder," throughout northwestern Mexico to facilitate yacht tourism in Mexico. A partial "land bridge," or widened highway, was built across the peninsula from Santa Rosalillita to the turnoff to Bahía de los Angeles. After the construction of a flawed marina at the Pacific fishing village of Santa Rosalillita, the plan was widely discredited and was cancelled in 2007.

Fish. A surfboard that is wider and shorter than traditional surfboards, usually with two fins and a swallowtail, often used for small-wave surfing.

Glassy. A condition favorable for surfing in which there is no wind and the surface of the ocean resembles a sheet of glass.

Hurley Pro. A professional surfing contest held annually in September at Lower Trestles in San Onofre State Beach in Southern California. The contest is sponsored by Hurley International, a surfwear company, and is the only U.S. mainland stop on the Association of Surfing Professionals World Tour.

June Gloom. Refers to the fact that the month of June in California can be a time in which coastal fog and clouds obscure the sun for days and even weeks at a time.

Kicking out. A surfing maneuver used at the end of riding a wave or to leave a wave that is closing out in which the surfer turns or "kicks" the surfboard out of the wave.

Kook. An insulting term for a surfer of poor ability and/or bad etiquette.

Lineup. An area beyond breaking waves where surfers congregate and wait for waves.

Luchador. A wrestler in the sport of lucha libre.

Lucha libre. The sport of Mexican wrestling.

Maquiladora. A factory or assembly plant located in the border region of Mexico.

Marea. The term for "tide" but also used to describe a fishing outing by fisherman in Baja California.

Narco. A person who engages in the illegal trade in narcotic drugs.

Narcocorrido. A drug ballad that emerged from the Mexican musical tradition of *corridos*. Narcocorridos often tell true stories of drug violence, arrests, and drug kingpins.

Narco-deco. A type of ornate architectural development in narco-financed construction found in border and drug regions of Mexico.

Palapa. A beach hut often constructed with a palm thatch roof.

Panga. A skiff or fiberglass fishing boat commonly used in the waters of Baja California.

Pointbreak. A surf break characterized by an extended point or headland off which waves break in a singular direction

Pueblito. A village.

Richard Hell. An iconic and pioneering New York punk rock singer involved with 1970s-era American punk bands such as Television, Heartbreakers, and later Richard Hell and the Voidoids.

Ripper. A surfer who rides, or "rips," waves well.

Rudo. A bad-guy wrestler in lucha libre who bends or breaks rules.

Salinera. A salt harvesting facility.

Set. A cluster of above-average-size waves. During a swell, waves will arrive at intervals in groups or sets.

Shorebreak. A type of surf spot or part of a surf break in which the wave breaks abruptly in shallow water along the shore.

Shoulder. The unbroken portion of a wave that is breaking.

Skeg. A term used in the longboard era for a fin on a surfboard.

Swell. Waves created by a common storm system that will occur over a defined period of time and are recognized as a measurable event (such as the Swell of 1969 or the Hurricane Swell of 1978).

Técnico. A good-guy wrestler in lucha libre.

Trestles. The famed surf area containing a series of cobblestone reef/points at the northern end of San Onofre State Beach. Trestles is one of the most popular and famous surfing areas in Southern California.

Tube ride. Surfing inside the barrel or hollow part of a wave.

Waterman. A well-rounded surfer in excellent physical condition who excels in all aspects of ocean sports such as bodysurfing, diving, and ocean lifesaving.

Notes

Introduction

1. William M. Denevan, "The Pristine Myth: The Landscape of the Americas in 1492," *Annals of the Association of American Geographers* 82, no. 3 (September 1992): 369.

2. For the way in which the photos by Eliot Porter depict a landscape void of people, see Joseph Wood Krutch, *Baja California and the Geography of Hope*, ed. Kenneth Brower (New York: Sierra Club and Ballantine Books, 1967). In contrast, Homer Aschmann's classic *The Central Desert of Baja California: Demography and Ecology* (Berkeley: University of California Press, 1959) documents the extensive historic human environmental impacts in the central desert of the Baja California peninsula.

3. For the history of piracy in Baja California, see Pablo L. Martínez, *Historia de Baja California* (1956; repr., La Paz: Consejo Editorial del Gobierno del Estado de B.C.S., 1991), ch. 7. For a summary of foreign leases and concessions to the peninsula, see Maria Luisa Garza, *El golfo de California, mar nacional* (Mexico City: Universidad Nacional Autónoma de México, 1976), ch. 7.

4. Angela Moyana, "William Walker en la península, 1853–1854," in *Baja California: Textos de su historia*, vol. 1, ed. Miguel Mathes, 202–24 (Mexico City: Instituto de Investigaciones Dr. Jose María Luis Mora, 1988).

5. Serge Dedina, *Saving the Gray Whale: People, Politics and Conservation in Baja California Sur, Mexico* (Tucson: University of Arizona Press, 2000), 24–25.

6. For a history of the formation of this fishing cooperative village and early coastal ejido, see Raul Arce and Francisco Sotero, *Punta Abreojos: 1948–1998* (Ensenada: Punta Abreojos Fishing Cooperative, 1998).

7. See Sandra Dibble and Lori Weisberg, "Baja's Building Boom," *San Diego Union-Tribune*, October 2, 2005, p. A1.

8. See "Sustainability" section at www.exploreloretobay.com. For the quotation from Bedsole, see Clinton Stark, "Breaking News: Loreto Bay Baja Resort, Unable to Find New Buyer, Suspends Operations," June 6, 2009, www.starksilvercreek.com. For information on FONATUR's management of Loreto

Bay, see Javier Chávez Davis, "Lograr que el proyecto Loreto Bay resurja es prioridad de FONATUR," *Sudcaliforniano*, January 15, 2010, www.oem.com.mx.

9. See Ginger Thompson, "Fighters for the Forests Are Released from Mexican Jail," *New York Times*, November 9, 2001, www.nytimes.com.

10. For a description of the trip, see Joe Sharkey, "A Radiant Coast of Mexico, Blighted by Drug Wars," *New York Times*, November 25, 2008, www.nytimes .com.

11. See Serge Dedina, "The New Face of Northern Mexico's Nature Preserves," *Borderlines* 43, no. 6 (1998), www.americas.irc-online.org.

12. Garth Murphy, *The Indian Lover* (New York: Simon and Schuster, 2002), 9.

13. Kem Nunn, lecture on *Tijuana Straits*, Tijuana Estuary Visitor's Center, Imperial Beach, California, September 1, 2004.

14. Kem Nunn, *The Tijuana Straits* (New York: Scribner, 2004), 41.

15. See Randy Olson, "Slow-Motion Disaster below the Waves," *Los Angeles Times*, November 17, 2002. See also the video documentary by the Shifting Baselines Ocean Media Project and the Surfrider Foundation, *Shifting Baselines in the Surf*, 2005, at www.shiftingbaselines.org.

16. For a description of my role in helping discover Mitsubishi's plan and the beginning of the campaign, see Dick Russell, *Eye of the Whale* (New York: Simon and Schuster, 2001), 82–85.

Part I. The Baja California Peninsula

1. See Richard Felger and Mary Beck Moser, *People of the Desert and Sea: Ethnobotany of the Seri Indians* (Tucson: University of Arizona Press, 1985).

2. According to Ben Finney and James D. Houston, "Kanaka is Hawaiian for person or human being. In the nineteenth century it came to mean a 'native person.'" Finney and Houston, *Surfing: An Ancient History of the Hawaiian Sport*, rev. ed. (Rohnert Park, CA: Pomegranate Artbooks, 1996), 100.

3. Charles Scammon, *The Marine Mammals of the North-western Coast of North America Described and Illustrated Together with an Account of the American Whale-Fishery* (1874; repr., New York: Dover, 1968), 261–62.

4. Echeverría quoted in Manuel Tello, *La política exterior de México (1970–1974)* (Mexico City: Fondo de Cultura Económica, 1975), 103.

5. Jorge Peon to President Ernesto Zedillo, April 20, 1995. Letter in author's possession.

6. Onell R. Soto, "Shipment of Liquefied Natural Gas Headed to Sempra Plant in Mexico," *San Diego Union-Tribune*, August 29, 2009, www.uniontrib.com.

7. See Victor M. Toledo, "The Ecological Consequences of the 1992 Agrarian Law of Mexico," in *Reforming Mexico's Agrarian Reform*, ed. Laura Randall, 247–70 (Armonk, NY: M. E. Sharpe, 1996); and María Teresa Vázquez Castillo, *Land Privatization in Mexico: Urbanization, Formation of Regions, and Globalization in Ejidos* (New York: Routledge, 2004).

8. For an example of how sewage is discharged onto the beach in northern Baja California, see Wildcoast, *Northern Baja Ocean Pollution*, video documentary, May 1, 2007, at www.youtube.com/wildcoast.

9. Irongate, "Trump Baja, Mexico Sells $120 Million of Residences in Day," press release, December 11, 2006, www.hotelsinteractive.com.

10. Dibble and Weisberg, "Baja's Building Boom."

11. See Laguna San Ignacio Conservation Alliance, "Laguna San Ignacio Conservation Plan," www.icfdn.org.

12. James C. McKinley Jr. "Mexican Land Boom Creates Commotion in Gray Whale Nursery," *New York Times*, March 12, 2006, p. A3.

Part II. The U.S.–Mexico Border

1. Serge Dedina, "The Geography of Transboundary Development in the Tijuana River Valley, 1920–1990," M.S. thesis, University of Wisconsin–Madison, 1991, 48–51.

2. For a description of the indigenous roots of lucha libre, see Lourdes Grobet, *Lucha Libre: Masked Superstars of Mexican Wrestling* (Mexico City: Trilce, 2008).

3. For a discussion of the political roots of punk rock, see Jon Savage, *England's Dreaming: Anarchy, Sex Pistols, Punk Rock, and Beyond* (New York: St. Martin's Griffin, 2001).

4. Project on Government Oversight, "The Politics of Contracting: Bajagua's No-Bid Deal," March 31, 2006, p. 1, www.pogo.org.

5. Scott J. Paltrow, "Smell Test: How Politics Influenced a Big Clean-up Deal," *Wall Street Journal*, January 29, 2007, p. 1.

6. S. D. Liddick, "A Sewer Runs Through It," *San Diego Magazine*, December 2007, www.sandiegomagazine.com.

7. United States Government Accountability Office, *International Boundary and Water Commission: Two Alternatives for Improving Wastewater Treatment at the United States–Mexico Border*, GAO-08-595R (Washington, DC: Government Accountability Office, 2009). See also Project on Government Oversight, "GAO Confirms That Bajagua Is a Stinky Deal," April 25, 2008, www.pogo.org.

8. Rob Davis, "Bajagua Project Killed," *Voice of San Diego*, May 16, 2008, www.voiceofsandiego.org.

Part III. Southern California

1. See Serge Dedina, *Saving the Gray Whale*, 57–59.

2. For a discussion of the conflicts over seals in La Jolla, see Martha Patricia Argomedo, "Antropología y naturaleza: El caso de un conflicto ambiental en La Jolla, California," Ph.D. diss., Universidad Nacional Autónoma de México, 2009.

3. California Senate Bill no. 428, July 20, 2009.

4. Matt McClain, "Surfrider Foundation's Final Thoughts on Recent Coastal Commission Decision," Surfrider Foundation press release, February 12, 2008.

5. Ibid.

Epilogue

1. For another view of this trip, see Kimball Taylor, "Wilderness Transect," *Surfer* (October 2009): 96–99, 140.

2. For detailed discussions of the skinny whale phenomenon, see Steven L. Swartz, "Changes in the Eastern North Pacific Gray Whale Population Status: A Monitoring Program for a 'Sentential' Population," National Marine Fisheries Service Draft ENP Gray Whale Monitoring, May 10, 2007; and Ken Weiss, "A Giant of the Sea Finds Slimmer Pickings," *Los Angeles Times*, July 6, 2007, www.latimes.com.

3. Joel Millman and Jim Carlton, "Plans for Mexico's Baja Face a Rough Landscape," *Wall Street Journal*, January 11, 2003, p. B1. For a comprehensive analysis of the demand for marina slips in Mexico, see EDAW, "Northwest Mexico Marina Market Analysis," a report prepared for the Packard Foundation, Los Altos, December 20, 2002.

4. Notimex, "Proponen investigar gestión de John McCarthy en Fonatur," April 29, 2008, www.noticias.terra.com.

5. See "Nevagua: A Solution for the Water Future of the Southwest and Baja California," March 2007, PowerPoint presentation; and Rob Davis, "Another Water Project for Bajagua Developer," *Voice of San Diego*, February 29, 2008, www.voiceofsandiego.org. As the Bajagua project started collapsing, Bajagua developer Enrique Landa promoted a proposal to build a desalination plant in Baja that involved complicated water "swaps" between the United States and Mexico.

6. Kevin B. Clark and his coauthors argue, "The vernal pools on Colonet mesa are unparalleled in northern Baja or Alta California . . . as varied and rich in species composition as all the remaining pools in southern California combined." Kevin B. Clark, Mark Dodero, Andreas Chavez, and Jonathan

Snapp-Cook, "The Threatened Biological Riches of Baja California's Colonet Mesa," *Fremontia* 36, no. 4 (2008): 4.

7. See United States Government Accountability Office, *Secure Border Initiative: Technology Deployment Delays Persist and the Impact of Border Fencing Has Not Been Assessed*, GAO-09-896 (Washington, DC: Government Accountability Office, 2009).

8. Sandra Dibble, "Every Drop Counts: Wastewater Recycling May Benefit Both Sides of the Border," *San Diego Union-Tribune*, July 6, 2009, www.uniontrib.com.

9. See Terrence Chea, "Sea Otters Could Return to Southern California," Associated Press, October 6, 2005, available at www.enn.com/wildlife/article/2775.

10. For an excellent overview of issues related to desalination in California, see Heather Cooley, Peter H. Gleick, and Gary Wolff, *Desalination with a Grain of Salt: A California Perspective* (Oakland, CA: Pacific Institute, 2006).

11. For a comprehensive review of the problems associated with sand replenishment projects in California and nationally, see United States Senate, *Washed Out to Sea: How Congress Prioritizes Beach Pork over National Needs*, Congressional Oversight and Investigation Report (Washington, DC: Office of Senator Tom Coburn, 2009).

Bibliography

Arce, Raul, and Francisco Sotero. *Punta Abreojos: 1948–1998*. Ensenada: Punta Abreojos Fishing Cooperative, 1998.

Argomedo, Martha Patricia. "Antropología y naturaleza: El caso de un conflicto ambiental en La Jolla, California." Ph.D. diss., Universidad Nacional Autónoma de México, 2009.

Aschmann, Homer. *The Central Desert of Baja California: Demography and Ecology*. Berkeley: University of California Press, 1959.

Chávez Davis, Javier. "Lograr que el proyecto Loreto Bay resurja es prioridad de FONATUR." *El Sudcaliforniano*, January 15, 2010. www.oem.com.mx/elsudcaliforniano/notas/n1479458.htm.

Chea, Terrence. "Sea Otters Could Return to Southern California." Associated Press, October 6, 2005. www.enn.com/wildlife/article/2775.

Clark, Kevin B., Mark Dodero, Andreas Chavez, and Jonathan Snapp-Cook. "The Threatened Biological Riches of Baja California's Colonet Mesa." *Fremontia* 36, no. 4 (2008): 3–10.

Cooley, Heather, Peter H. Gleick, and Gary Wolff. *Desalination with a Grain of Salt: A California Perspective*. Oakland, CA: Pacific Institute, 2006.

Davis, Rob. "Another Water Project for Bajagua Developer." *Voice of San Diego*, February 29, 2008. www.voiceofsandiego.org.

———. "Bajagua Project Killed." *Voice of San Diego*, May 16, 2008. www.voiceofsandiego.org.

Dedina, Serge. "The Geography of Transboundary Development in the Tijuana River Valley, 1920–1990." M.S. thesis, University of Wisconsin–Madison, 1991.

———. "The New Face of Northern Mexico's Nature Preserves." *Borderlines* 43, no. 6 (1998), www.americas.irc-online.org.

———. *Saving the Gray Whale: People, Politics and Conservation in Baja California Sur, Mexico*. Tucson: University of Arizona Press, 2000.

Denevan, William M. "The Pristine Myth: The Landscape of the Americas in 1492." *Annals of the Association of American Geographers* 82, no. 3 (September 1992): 369–85.

Dibble, Sandra. "Every Drop Counts: Wastewater Recycling May Benefit Both Sides of the Border." *San Diego Union-Tribune*, July 6, 2009. www.uniontrib .com.

Dibble, Sandra, and Lori Weisberg. "Baja's Building Boom." *San Diego Union-Tribune*, October 2, 2005. www.uniontrib.com.

EDAW. "Northwest Mexico Marina Market Analysis." Report prepared for the Packard Foundation, Los Altos, California, December 20, 2002.

Felger, Richard, and Mary Beck Moser. *People of the Desert and Sea: Ethnobotany of the Seri Indians*. Tucson: University of Arizona Press, 1985.

Finney, Ben, and James D. Houston. *Surfing: An Ancient History of the Hawaiian Sport*. Rev. ed. Rohnert Park, CA: Pomegranate Artbooks, 1996.

Garza, Maria Luisa. *El golfo de California, mar nacional*. Mexico City: Universidad Nacional Autónoma de México, 1976.

Grobet, Lourdes. *Lucha Libre: Masked Superstars of Mexican Wrestling*. Mexico City: Trilce, 2008.

Krutch, Joseph Wood. *Baja California and the Geography of Hope*. Edited by Kenneth Brower, with a foreword by David Brower. New York: Sierra Club and Ballantine Books, 1967.

Liddick, S. D. "A Sewer Runs Through It." *San Diego Magazine*, December 2007. www.sandiegomagazine.com.

Martínez, Pablo L. *Historia de Baja California*. 1956. Repr., La Paz: Consejo Editorial del Gobierno del Estado de B.C.S., 1991.

McKinley, James C., Jr. "Mexican Land Boom Creates Commotion in Gray Whale Nursery." *New York Times*, March 12, 2006, p. A3.

Millman, Joel, and Jim Carlton. "Plans for Mexico's Baja Face a Rough Landscape." *Wall Street Journal*, January 11, 2003, p. B1.

Moyana, Angela. "William Walker en la península, 1853–1854." In *Baja California: Textos de su historia*, vol. 1, edited by Miguel Mathes, 202–24. Mexico City: Instituto de Investigaciones Dr. Jose María Luis Mora, 1988.

Murphy, Garth. *The Indian Lover*. New York: Simon and Schuster, 2002.

Notimex. "Proponen investigar gestión de John McCarthy en Fonatur." April 29, 2008. www.noticias.terra.com.

Nunn, Kem. *The Tijuana Straits*. New York: Scribner, 2004.

Olson, Randy. "Slow-Motion Disaster below the Waves." *Los Angeles Times*, November 17, 2002. www.latimes.com.

Paltrow, Scot J. "Smell Test: How Politics Influenced a Big Clean-up Deal." *Wall Street Journal*, January 29, 2007, p. A1.

Project on Government Oversight. "GAO Confirms That Bajagua Is a Stinky Deal." April 25, 2008. www.pogo.org.

———. "The Politics of Contracting: Bajagua's No-Bid Deal." March 31, 2006. www.pogo.org.

Russell, Dick. *Eye of the Whale*. New York: Simon and Schuster, 2001.

Savage, Jon. *England's Dreaming: Anarchy, Sex Pistols, Punk Rock, and Beyond*. New York: St. Martin's Griffin, 2001.

Scammon, Charles. *The Marine Mammals of the North-western Coast of North America Described and Illustrated Together with an Account of the American Whale-Fishery*. 1874. Repr., with introduction by Victor B. Scheffer, New York: Dover, 1968.

Sharkey, Joe. "A Radiant Coast of Mexico, Blighted by Drug Wars." *New York Times*, November 25, 2008. www.nytimes.com.

Shifting Baselines Ocean Media Project and the Surfrider Foundation. *Shifting Baselines in the Surf*. Video documentary. 2005. www.shiftingbaselines.org.

Soto, Onell R. "Shipment of Liquefied Natural Gas Headed to Sempra Plant in Mexico." *San Diego Union-Tribune*, August 29, 2009. www.uniontrib .com.

Stark, Clinton. "Breaking News: Loreto Bay Baja Resort, Unable to Find New Buyer, Suspends Operations." June 6, 2009. www.starksilvercreek.com/2009/06/ breaking-news-loreto-bay-construction-suspended-notice-operations-bankrupt.html.

Swartz, Steven L. "Changes in the Eastern North Pacific Gray Whale Population Status: A Monitoring Program for a 'Sentential' Population." National Marine Fisheries Service Draft ENP Gray Whale Monitoring, May 10, 2007.

Taylor, Kimball. "Wilderness Transect." *Surfer*, October 2009, pp. 96–99, 140.

Tello, Manuel. *La política exterior de México (1970–1974)*. Mexico City: Fondo de Cultura Económica, 1975.

Thompson, Ginger. "Fighters for the Forests Are Released from Mexican Jail." *New York Times*, November 9, 2001. www.nytimes.com.

Toledo, Victor M. "The Ecological Consequences of the 1992 Agrarian Law of Mexico." In *Reforming Mexico's Agrarian Reform*, edited by Laura Randall, 247–70. Armonk, NY: M. E. Sharpe, 1996.

United States Government Accountability Office. *International Boundary and Water Commission: Two Alternatives for Improving Wastewater Treatment at the United States–Mexico Border*. GAO-08-595R. Washington, DC: Government Accountability Office, April 24, 2009.

———. *Secure Border Initiative: Technology Deployment Delays Persist and the Impact of Border Fencing Has Not Been Assessed*. GAO-09-896. Washington, DC: Government Accountability Office, September 9, 2009.

United States Senate. *Washed Out to Sea: How Congress Prioritizes Beach Pork over National Needs.* Congressional Oversight and Investigation Report. Washington, DC: Office of Senator Tom Coburn, May 2009.

Vázquez Castillo, María Teresa. *Land Privatization in Mexico: Urbanization, Formation of Regions, and Globalization in Ejidos.* New York: Routledge, 2004.

Warshaw, Matt. *The Encyclopedia of Surfing.* Orlando, FL: Harcourt, 2003.

Weiss, Ken. "A Giant of the Sea Finds Slimmer Pickings: Gray Whales Are Skinnier, and Scientists Suspect Arctic Warming Is the Reason Why." *Los Angeles Times,* July 6, 2007. www.latimes.com.

Wildcoast. *Northern Baja Ocean Pollution.* Video documentary, May 1, 2007. www.youtube.com/wildcoast.

Index

About the Author

S erge Dedina is the cofounder and executive director of Wildcoast, a binational nonprofit organization with offices in Imperial Beach, California, and Ensenada, Mexico, that conserves coastal and marine ecosystems and wildlife. He initiated an international campaign that successfully stopped the Mitsubishi Corporation from destroying San Ignacio Lagoon. The *Wall Street Journal, Washington Post, New York Times, Christian Science Monitor, Surfer Magazine, USA Today, Los Angeles Times, Chicago Tribune, NBC Nightly News, The Today Show*, National Public Radio, CNN, and CBS News have all reported on Serge's coastal conservation activities. For his role in helping to protect the coastline of the Californias, Serge received the Surf Industry Manufacturer's Association "Environmentalist of the Year" Award, the San Diego Zoological Society's Conservation Medal, and the "Coastal Hero" Award from the California Coastal Commission, and *Sunset Magazine*.

Serge is the author of *Saving the Gray Whale* (University of Arizona Press), a book based on the three years he lived at the gray whale lagoons of Baja California. His articles on coastal issues and surfing have been published in the *Journal of Borderlands Studies, Los Angeles Times, San Diego Union-Tribune, Surfline, Surfers Journal, Voice of San Diego, Longboard Magazine, Surfshot, Orange County Voice, Grist, California Coast and Ocean*, and *San Diego News Network*.

Serge received a doctorate in geography from the University of Texas at Austin. He also holds a master's degree in geography from the University of Wisconsin and a bachelor's degree in political science from the University of California, San Diego.

Serge has lived and surfed in Mexico, Peru, El Salvador, France, Spain, England, and Morocco. Today, Imperial Beach, California, located just across the border from Mexico, is Serge's base. It is where he rescued more than five hundred people while working as an ocean lifeguard and helped save the Tijuana Estuary from development. Today, he directs Wildcoast from an office across from the Imperial Beach pier. When he's not exploring the back roads of Baja California, Serge can be found at the beach with his wife, Emily, and surfing with his two sons, Daniel and Israel.